Paris
Undressed

Paris Undressed

THE SECRETS OF FRENCH LINGERIE

KATHRYN KEMP-GRIFFIN
ILLUSTRATIONS BY PALOMA CASILE

AMBROSIA

Published in Canada in 2016 by House of Anansi Press Inc.
www.houseofanansi.com

House of Anansi Press is committed to protecting our natural environment.
As part of our efforts, the interior of this book is printed on paper that contains
100% post-consumer recycled fibres, is acid-free, and is processed chlorine-free.

20 19 18 17 16   1 2 3 4 5

Library and Archives Canada Cataloguing in Publication

Kemp-Griffin, Kathryn, author
Paris undressed: the secrets of French lingerie / Kathryn Kemp-Griffin;
illustrated by Paloma Casile.

Issued in print and electronic formats.
ISBN: 978-1-4870-0063-9 (hardback). ISBN: 978-1-4870-0064-6 (pdf).

1.Lingerie. 2.Lingerie — France — Paris. I.Casile, Paloma, illustrator
II.Title.

TT670.K46 2016 687'.22 C2016-901814-8
C2016-901815-6

Cover and text design: Alysia Shewchuk
Cover illustration: Paloma Casile

We acknowledge for their financial support of our publishing program
the Canada Council for the Arts, the Ontario Arts Council, and the Government
of Canada through the Canada Book Fund.

Printed and bound in Canada

For all the women who have ever wanted
more from their lingerie

CONTENTS

A NEW BEGINNING

HEADS OR TAILS?

*Let your dream devour your life so that your
life doesn't devour your dream.*
—*Antoine de Saint-Exupéry*

American women wear underwear. French women wear lingerie.

French women seem to be born with the ability to inhabit their lives and bodies with effortless grace and sensuality. What's their secret?

Lingerie.

In America it's all about the gift-with-purchase, getting more for less, or splurging, but in France lingerie reflects an *art de vivre*, a philosophy dedicated to an enhanced well-being.

Take, for example, your bra. A good one not only shapes how others see us, it shapes how we see ourselves. What bra do you have on right now? Not sure? Then keep reading. This book cracks the code of the *je ne sais quoi* of French lingerie — how to buy it, wear it, and use it to help gain outward poise and inner confidence.

Paris Undressed will help you cultivate a lingerie wardrobe that will have you living fully in the sensuality of the moment, no matter the occasion. It combines the practical (how to choose a bra and get the perfect fit) with the sublime (how to appreciate and wear lingerie as art). In short, this book is the culmination of everything I have learned and the result of more than twenty years of my experience, observations, and conversations about life, love, and lingerie.

I know what you're thinking. I'm not an Inès or a Céline. What can a Canadian named Kate possibly know about French lingerie?

Twenty years ago, admittedly, not much. I came to France wearing faded Jockey For Her cotton panties whose shredded elastic floated like tentacles on a jellyfish. No one could accuse me of being a savvy lingerie-wearer. What was I even doing in France?

Let's rewind.

Heads, Paris. Tails, San Francisco. That's how my husband and I decided to change our lives — by coin toss.

It was a hot July night in 1990. Christian and I were sitting on our back porch in Toronto, sipping through the froth of our cold Molson Canadians and contemplating our lives together. Everything was perfect. Maybe *too* perfect. We had recently celebrated our first wedding anniversary and bought our first house together. Our careers were blossoming. No children yet, but we certainly wanted a family. Everything was going according to plan.

Hence the problem. Neither of us wanted to look back from the vantage point of our fiftieth wedding anniversary and say,

"Well, that went exactly as expected."

No longer content to settle for the certainty of the familiar, we dared destiny.

"Let's take a sabbatical," I suggested.

"Sure," said Christian. "The first one of us to make a million dollars gets to choose where we spend it."

"We don't need a million," I said. "We could leave tomorrow if we wanted. Just take off. Find jobs somewhere else."

Maybe it was the heat or the thrill of the adventure. More likely it was the beer.

Christian brought out an atlas, closed his eyes, and pointed to a spot on a page. When he opened them, his finger was on Chile. We could imagine ourselves hiking the Andes.

I watched as Christian's fingers skittered over the world: Sydney, Tokyo, Lagos, Novosibirsk — although we both agreed we would not be moving to the capital of Siberia any time soon.

We continued our game of Twister using the world as our floor print. As the game accelerated, so did our excitement. We finally narrowed our choices in a more serious way to San Francisco or Paris.

It was hard to hide my preference. I had always been in love with France — the country and the culture — but mostly I loved the language, despite my poor grasp of it. Living in Canada requires a minimal knowledge of French, given that it's an official language, and I had worked for a summer as an au pair in the Loire Valley and spent a year studying in Grenoble. Yet all I could do was count to a hundred and order *mousse au chocolat* for dessert. In spite of the linguistic challenges, there was no denying the magnetic pull of the City of Light. I longed to live, eat, breathe, and maybe even dream in French.

That day in 1990, Christian and I had one coin and two choices: San Francisco with its byte-sized Silicon Valley promises, or Paris with its bite-sized, Michelin-starred *amuse-bouches*. Christian tossed the quarter high in the air, giving it some spin; our destiny twirled and glinted above us.

When the coin landed on Paris, I was beyond excited. I was *folle de joie*, crazy with happiness. Our French adventure was about to begin.

A PARISIAN AWAKENING

THE ART OF LIVING

~

Paris: the lingerie capital of the world

ONE

AN INVITATION TO THE SENSES

Paris. Paris. There is something silken and elegant about that word, something carefree, something made for a dance, something brilliant and festive, like champagne. Everything there is beautiful, gay, and a little drunk, and festooned with lace.
— Nina Berberova

Paris is a city that takes its time — especially when you're in a hurry.

Tourists blame the Parisians, Parisians blame the tourists, and everybody blames the traffic. Or the strikes. Or the holidays. Despite the finger-wagging, however, there is tolerance — and delight — in the City of Light for those who learn to expect the unexpected. Paris is a celebration of unhurried time, an invitation to discover and tease your senses. Like a kiss at dawn that longs for nightfall, Paris is best lived not by tallying what you pack into a day, but by what you manage to stretch out over the course of it.

Paris is a small big city. Geographically speaking, it occupies only 105 square kilometres of the earth's surface, which is not much compared to other major cities and popular tourist destinations. New York is eight times larger, and London and Bangkok both sprawl over fifteen times the space. In terms of population, the two million inhabitants in the French capital pales in comparison to the more than eight million in each of those three other cities.

But small numbers add up. Rather, they multiply exponentially, placing Paris high on the population density charts with an average of twenty-one people per square kilometre compared to New York's ten, or London and Bangkok's average of five. Building-height restrictions in Paris have prevented people from piling up and encouraged them to spill out onto the streets.

Whether you prefer the company of others or the solitude of anonymity, *les rues* of Paris invite us to engage. A vibrant café culture encourages conversation and debate while winding cobblestone pathways nestled between broad boulevards give the freedom to wander and lose your way, knowing you'll never be truly lost. This overlapping of lives and experiences heightens the senses and makes everything feel more intimate and more immediate.

Four weeks after the coin landed, Christian and I had quit our jobs, put our house on the market, broken the news to our stunned yet supportive relatives, and were on a plane to Paris. We stayed temporarily in a boutique hotel where mornings began in a breakfast room overlooking an inner courtyard. There were hardwood floors, teal velvet chairs, ivory damask table linens, hammered metal flatware, along with freshly squeezed orange juice, a basket brimming with hot-from-the-baker's-oven croissants, and café au lait in wide, vintage bowls. My breakfasts in Canada had been eaten over the sink and washed down with coffee to go. In Paris, I could have lingered over *petit déjeuner* all day.

But I had work to do. Christian had secured a fashionable job on the European team of Polo Ralph Lauren, which generously included these temporary accommodations until we could find a place of our own. While he worked in their flagship store at place de la Madeleine, I scoured newspapers and bulletin boards in churches and community centres looking for a job and an apartment. Days and weeks passed. Apartments within our budget were as scarce as jobs that included working papers. Not being able to roll my *r*'s didn't help either, but I remained optimistic, confident that a combination of luck, effort, and the magic of Paris would help me along.

The best way to get to know a city is to walk it, and I didn't need much convincing to hit the streets. By day I walked and by night I charted and planned my route to maximize efficiency. One day, I decided to walk across Paris. Literally. At a good pace, I figured I could cover the fourteen-kilometre journey from Porte Maillot to Bois de Vincennes in about three hours. I set out from the hotel in my running shoes, hauling an oversized knapsack packed with a picnic lunch, water, gum, sunscreen, sweater, *Plan de Paris*, and a leather-bound journal

I had received as a going-away present. Looking back, I was more appropriately dressed for trekking in the mountains than a promenade through the birthplace of the little black dress.

It started to drizzle as I made my way around the Arc de Triomphe and started down the Champs-Élysées. I had everything in my backpack except an umbrella, and by the time I reached place de la Concorde, the drizzle had turned to pelting rain. Hurried by an irresistible impulse, I sought refuge in Angelina, a prestigious tearoom steeped — or stuck — in *belle époque* grandeur. The hostess scowled and I smiled through the water dripping off my bangs. It was only when I sat down and saw my reflection in the opulent wall mirror that I noticed the real source of her disdain. My soaked, clingy, see-through T-shirt exposed the veteran sports bra I wore on days like this — days that didn't matter, days where nobody was supposed to see it. I pulled the sweater from my knapsack and draped it around my shoulders to conceal my embarrassment and then did what everybody else did *chez* Angelina: I ordered their famous molten hot chocolate, which arrived in a ceramic pitcher accompanied by a billowing pot of whipped cream.

Real chocolate. Real cream. Real china.

Time unravelled as I sat there, soggy, yet stilled in the moment.

The rain had subsided by the time I was finished. I crossed rue de Rivoli to walk through the Tuileries, a landscape garden built on proportion, symmetry, and grace that stretches from place de la Concorde to the Louvre. Once reserved for royalty and members of the court, the Tuileries became one of the first public gardens in Paris and continues to welcome both locals and tourists wishing to stroll its pathways lined with centuries-old chestnut trees. There is nothing quite like the fresh, earthy fragrance after a rainfall: I inhaled its bounty.

Blue skies gradually appeared and the sun dried the chalky gravel of the pathways. Once I reached the Louvre, my running shoes were coated. I brushed off what I could and walked up to rue Saint-Honoré, one of the most luxurious and fashionable streets in Paris. Women walked by in maxi dresses, crisp linen trousers, nautical stripes, floral prints, and signature bags. Had we been through the same rainstorm? Even the mannequins seemed to furrow their brows at my sodden sartorial look.

Bailing on my original itinerary, I spontaneously headed toward the pedestrian bridge, pont des Arts, and found solace in the sounds of a jazz quartet in rhythm with the late morning sunlight dancing on the Seine. Street artists and musicians are everywhere in Paris. Whether in the metro, under arches, on bridges, steps, or corners, artistic interludes are part of the Parisian landscape. The soft wail of a saxophone faded behind me as I continued my walk along the Seine and through Île de la Cité and Île Saint-Louis, two tiny islands that make up the heart of Paris. Both are charming, but the smaller Île Saint-Louis has the added distinction of being home to Berthillon, the best ice cream parlour in the city.

I had intended to walk right by Berthillon, but the sight of two girls giggling while tasting each other's sorbet changed my mind. I crossed the bridge behind Notre Dame cathedral and got in line. There is always a line at Berthillon, but it didn't matter; I needed the time to consider the myriad flavours. I picked *sorbet cassis* and my tongue tingled from the first lick — a tart and refreshing contrast to the sun warming my face. By now I had completely forgotten about the path I had mapped out for myself and just kept walking east.

At place de la Bastille, I left the crowds on street level and climbed the stairs to the Promenade Plantée, a planted walkway built on top of an abandoned railroad running over a viaduct. Neither a rooftop *terrasse* nor a ground-level garden, this raised path, approximately the height of a third floor, offered an opportunity to see the city from another dimension. Today the walkway includes footbridges and tunnels and extends four and a half kilometres to Bois de Vincennes, but back in the early nineties, landscaping had only begun. I walked as long as I could and looked out over the vistas along the way.

Back at street level, I continued down avenue Daumesnil until a looming labyrinth of roadways indicated the eastern city limits. Cars roared above me on the Périphérique, the ring road that circles Paris, and echoed and reverberated as I made my way through the concrete corridor to the other side, where I was greeted by the verdant border of Bois de Vincennes.

I'd made it. Triumphant.

And hungry.

I sat under a tree on the bank of lac Daumesnil, a lake in the woods, and took out my *jambon-beurre* sandwich. Available everywhere, *jambon-beurre* is the French equivalent to fast food. I had been quick to judge this seemingly lacking sandwich the first time I'd tried it. Ham and butter on baguette — that's it?

Yes, there are only three ingredients, the butter so vital it beats out "baguette" in the name.

While Americans go to great lengths to emphasize that a recipe is made without butter, the French are busy specifying which kind to use: *beurre doux* (unsalted) or *beurre salé* (salted). The difference is big. Salted butter enhances taste and brings out the subtlety of flavours. Try it with three pieces of bread. No butter on the first, unsalted on the second, and salted on the third. Add a piece of ham or cheese.

Taste, taste, and taste again.

In France, it's never too early to learn to appreciate food. Guess where you would find the following menu?

Asperges sauce vinaigrette – Asparagus with vinaigrette
Confit de canard – Duck confit
Haricots tarbais – Tarbais beans
Tomme noire – Tomme cheese
Fruit de saison – Seasonal fruit

A world-renowned gastronomic Parisian establishment? *Pas du tout*. This epicurean experience is a typical lunch menu at a public primary school. These kids don't get their food from a lunchbox or a greasy grill. Children are served an *entrée, plat et dessert* (appetizer, main dish, and dessert), and even three-year-olds are required to bring their own *serviette de table*, cloth napkin, to school along with their crayons. Weekly menus are posted for parents to see and discuss with their children. A national program in primary schools, *La Semaine du Goût*, dedicates a full week to teaching youngsters how to distinguish among sweet, sour, salty, and bitter.

Tuning the taste buds early is the first step toward learning how to pair foods, which will enhance the enjoyment of food throughout life, but a fine palate isn't the only thing that gets cultivated early in France. The cultivation of pleasure — recognizing it and knowing what brings delight — isn't considered self-indulgent but rather as essential to living a full life. Life is richer when experienced through the layers of all five senses — sight, smell, sound, taste, and touch. For the French, enjoying the senses is as natural as breathing, and is imperative to the quality of any experience, large or small. I had only scraped the surface of the senses on my walk. What started as a journey from A to B relaxed into a sensorial experience and discovery of the extent to which senses can trigger and engage our whole body.

I lost track of time in the Bois de Vincennes as I filled my journal with *pensées*: thoughts, notes, vocabulary, and expressions. It had been a surprising journey of insight, one I wanted to continue and nurture. I resolved to treat each day like a treasure hunt, collecting sights, sounds, smells, tastes, and textures, and to use my journal as a place to record and reflect my new sensory discoveries.

On my way back to the hotel, I took a detour to see an apartment in the heart of the fifteenth arrondissement. It was slightly over our budget, but I decided it wouldn't hurt to look.

I smelled the cherry blossoms as soon as I exited the Pasteur metro station. I looked around. The gold dome of the Invalides and the Tour Eiffel rose in the distance. Freshly baked baguettes from the *boulangerie* were tucked beneath arms, pyramids of cheese beckoned from the *fromagerie*, and flowers spilled onto the sidewalk of the *fleuriste*. The apartment itself was a sunny sixth-floor walk-up (127 steps, to be precise) with three spacious rooms that overlooked a courtyard on one side and a garden with artist lofts on the other. No elevator. No dishwasher. But I didn't care. I loved it. It was *chez nous*.

Euphoric, I floated down the stairs and out on to the sidewalk, almost colliding with the florist. Inspired, perhaps, by all the gardens I had seen, I selected a bouquet of peonies in a *camaïeu* of pinks with each petal singing its scent. The florist asked me if the flowers were *pour offrir*, to give. No, I told her, they were just for me. Nevertheless, she carefully wrapped the composition in a layer of diaphanous tissue paper and kraft with loops of raffia to hold it in place. Imagine to what lengths she would have gone if it had been a gift!

Customer service in my new city was less about easy returns and more about harnessing delight. Business was less about location, location, location, and more about sensation, sensation, sensation. Christian and I had made the right coin toss. Now all I needed was a new bra.

TWO

CARESS THE NOW

The eyes caress more sweetly than the lips.
— Auguste Angellier

I used to be one of those women who only bought a new bra when the washing machine ripped the old one to shreds. A bra was a basic necessity. Functional and nothing more.

But now that I was in Paris, it was time for a new beginning, a change in habits — a new me! I pledged that I would refresh my lingerie and my attitude. Goodbye tattered bra... hello — well, what exactly?

Lingerie stores are everywhere in Paris, including just down the street from our new digs. The sign above the boutique said Lingerie Annabelle. As I pushed open the door marked *entrée libre*, a shrill bell announced my entrance into a space no larger than a birdcage. I was greeted with an officious "Bonjour, Madame" and a terse smile from the woman behind the counter — Annabelle, I presumed.

As the bell continued to chime like a theft alarm because I hadn't closed the door properly behind me, I stammered with my bad accent, *"Un soutien-gorge, s'il vous plait."* A bra, please.

"Avec ou sans dentelle?" Madame Annabelle asked. What did she want to know? I flipped through my pocket Larousse to discover that *dentelle* meant lace. With or without lace, she had asked.

Was I a lace person? I had no clue.

Madame Annabelle pulled out an ivory satin bra with small pleats that was trimmed in lace. She ushered me into a minuscule changing room where she deftly adjusted the back hooks and tightened the straps, running her fingers over the bra like she was tuning a violin. She handed me *une culotte assortie*, a matching panty, indicating that I should put it on. Now. I hadn't even asked for panties.

When I turned to face the mirror, I couldn't believe what I saw. I'm five foot seven, but...had I suddenly grown taller? My back was straighter. My breasts were lifted and fuller-looking. And what was that on my face?

A smile.

Normally, I found shopping for any kind of lingerie a miserable experience, complete with cheesy marketing, loud music, and bad lighting. During one visit to a lingerie megastore in New York City, I was so dazed by the towering panty pyramid and the "Buy 3 Get 1 FREE!" neon sign that I went for the same look as the decked-out mannequin beside me. The teddy scratched a little, but the effervescent saleswoman promised that it wouldn't stay on long enough to bother me. She also managed to talk me into buying a Pamper Me Kit, complete with shower gel, exfoliating glove, body lotion, and headband. It made for a night to remember, but for all the wrong reasons. What a production! I felt like I'd hosted a sit-down dinner for twelve, and couldn't wait to be back in my favourite T-shirt.

This was a different experience. Madame Annabelle was quiet and patient. She understood that it takes a while to adjust to what you see in the mirror, to grasp the simple message of quiet beauty. I didn't feel the pressure of having to be — or pretending to be — someone who was likely to jump out of a centerfold at a sperm bank.

Lingerie doesn't always need an ulterior motive. With Madame Annabelle, I felt at ease to appreciate the beauty of a very good bra. I wanted to feel like this every day.

My confidence swelled. Madame Annabelle observed quietly, like a mother deer watching her fawn learn to stand. Her silence gave me time to experience and appreciate a sensation I had never felt before, an awakening. It felt like a day brimming with promise.

I still have that first pleated bra, although it has long since retired from service. When I open my drawer in the morning, those gentle folds make me pause and remember that I have a choice: I can have an ordinary day or an extraordinary one.

I'm sure that when Madame Annabelle helped me, she didn't realize she was setting in motion a seismic shift in my appreciation of lingerie, a shift that would engender both a passion and a career. Within months, I'd started my own company, Soyelle, specializing in lingerie accessories and beauty products. You might think I had no business starting a lingerie company in the lingerie capital of the world. After all, I had only just bought my first real bra. But, while the French certainly knew how to design beautiful lingerie, caring for it remained problematic. With the help of a chemist, I developed a delicate fabric wash, and Soyelle was born.

Many years later, I sold that company, but in the meantime I noticed a pronounced difference between how women of different nationalities viewed their lingerie. American women needed guidance. I began to conduct lingerie tours of Paris to help navigate the silk contours of the French capital. These tours are more than a shopping expedition. My aim is to help women enjoy a renewed sense of femininity, confidence, and elegance.

On these tours, I inevitably hear women make one, if not both, of these two comments: "I need to lose a couple of pounds first" and "Who's going to see it anyway?" There's a tendency to try to justify lingerie choices, with women preferring to spend money on a dress that everyone will see rather than on something very few might. When women do decide to spend, we use words like *splurge* and *indulge*, as if feeling good is the exception rather than the rule. Thinking of lingerie in terms of conditions to fill — the when, how, where, and why — takes all the fun out of it.

In America, women save their best lingerie for date night or Valentine's Day. French women don't need a special occasion — or permission. They resist cookie-cutter definitions and labels for love. Dinner with a love interest isn't a "date" or "a special occasion," because every occasion is one to savour, not save for.

Why put a quota on pleasure? If lingerie feels good next to your skin, why not wear it as much as possible? *Life* is the special occasion. Today. Right here. Right now.

Intrinsic to the French is the expression *joie de vivre*, suggesting an inherent love of and zest for life. In English, it translates as "joy of living," which isn't quite the same thing, but then again, that expression hails from a land that needs a book to rejoice in the joy of sex.

The French don't need books to tell them how to enjoy sex or life. All of that is already accessible, like jasmine inviting you to inhale its intoxicating scent, or the *millefeuille* in a patisserie inviting you into its layered decadence: *c'est que du bonheur*, it's pure happiness. You just need to reach out for it.

French women see lingerie as a catalyst for sensations, a way to connect and integrate the fullness of any moment, whereas Americans see lingerie along a line spectrum. At one end is "special" lingerie for highly anticipated and deserving moments; at the other is "comfortable"— lingerie for low-energy, everyday moments, like sitting in baggy sweatpants. No wonder it's impossible to imagine "special" and "comfortable" coexisting!

Let's take a closer look at these words we use to describe our lingerie experiences. In English, *special* means unique, exceptional, and invaluable, while in French, *spécial* suggests something peculiar, odd, or unconventional. Describing someone as *spécial* won't get you a dinner invitation. Paradoxically, the expression *c'est normal*, it's normal, suggests an ordinary expectedness. For the French, *c'est normal* is to find pleasure and enjoyment in everything around you: a posy of wild flowers, an extra ten minutes facing the sun on the terrace, and wearing beautiful lingerie because it feels divine, not because it's Valentine's Day.

The word *comfortable* gets used to justify the overstretched panties at the bottom of the drawer. ("But they're so comfortable!") Those panties — and all the faded bras surrounding them — are more likely deserving of another adjective: *sloppy*.

The line between comfortable and sloppy blurs when the discussion is no longer about enhancing your well-being. Think of comfort in terms of providing a benefit to how you feel, rather than as relief from discomfort — because comfort is not a zero-sum game, and it is not the only criterion by which to judge lingerie.

As with *La Semaine du Goût*, an appreciation for lingerie is an education that begins with the purchase of a girl's first bra. The French understand that there is nothing more disappointing than when deception lands on their tongue — or on their skin.

I remember how very proud my mother was the day we went shopping for my first bra. I was not. I didn't want anything to do with breasts or other curves. It didn't help that the lingerie section of the department store was next to the jeans. All I could think about was that my sixth-grade unrequited love interest would be shopping for Levis with his friends while I was trying on training bras — "training," like I had just joined the reserves. My girlfriends recounted similar stories of fear, dread, and uncertainty in connection with the purchase of their first bra.

Curious to know about first bra stories in France, I asked French lingerie designers to share their memories. Their spontaneous and candid responses shed light on some of the mystery surrounding this common though rarely discussed experience. Here's what they had to say.

Patricia Cadolle, heir to a family lingerie legacy, remembers her first bra being a Cadolle (*bien sûr!*) that was extremely refined, embroidered tulle.

A very thoughtful saleswoman helped Laetitia Schlumberger, the designer of Lingerie Dement, select a white piqué balconnette bra with inlays of white flowers in tulle that she still has — twenty-three years later. And Paloma Casile, the illustrator of this book, still has her first bra, too: a powder pink bra with delicate embroidery.

Caroline Tannous of Les Jupons de Tess had a lot of fun choosing shapes and designs and bought "an ivory lace bra from princesse tam tam that was youthful and innocent." Elise Raphalen, of Elise Aucouturier, also selected princesse tam tam for her first bra, which was a Scottish plaid print with a small ribbon of dark red velvet.

Jina Luciani from occidente bought a triangle bra made of cotton with a lace detail that "felt poetic and gentle" next to her skin, and Charline Goutal, the creative talent of Ma P'tite Culotte will never forget trying on her first bra and seeing "how lingerie can express a mood and accentuate a personality trait."

What do you remember about your first bra? What did it look like? How did it make you feel?

SPECIAL *AND* COMFORTABLE:
HOW TO HAVE BOTH

Lingerie should feel accessible, not abstract and precious. It's all about triggering sensations and creating new habits so that you thrill to your lingerie instead of making excuses for it. I wondered what else might change if my perspective shifted. I began to jot down lingerie vocabulary and expressions and reflections on what lingerie meant to me. My journal became my lingerie journal. An evolution was in progress. I could feel it.

For the French, good lingerie is always visually pleasing, and always comfortable — so comfortable that you wouldn't think of wearing anything else. Here are six reflections that helped me integrate both comfort and aesthetics into my lingerie wardrobe:

1. Start using the word *lingerie* instead of the truly uninspiring *underwear*. You have a *lingerie* drawer and you're wearing *lingerie* right now.

2. Reserve the words *indulge* and *empower* for describing chocolate and equal rights — anything except your lingerie! Instead, try to *cultivate* and *curate* when making lingerie decisions, and describe your collection as *lovely*, *exquisite*, *soft*, or *sublime*.

3. If you don't already have a scented sachet in your lingerie drawer, try adding wrapped guest soap for an inexpensive and elegant olfactory touch. The scent will encourage a vivid emotional association with your lingerie.

4. Wear everything in your lingerie drawer (but not all at once!). Do it over the next couple of weeks, without cheating by going back to your favourites. Anything you can't bring yourself to wear has no place in your drawer, or your life. Time to toss, donate, or start charging rent. (You'll learn how to build your lingerie collection later in the book.)

5. Buy a single flower in the colour of your favourite bra. Notice that there are no flowers in beige! If that's the only colour in your lingerie selection, buy a flower in your favourite colour, and buy a bra in that colour, too.

6. Say goodbye to "everyday" lingerie. There's nothing "everyday" about every day of your life. Remember how

important you felt when you penned your signature for the first time, and how unique you feel every time you sign it? Developing your own lingerie signature feels the same way. Lingerie by definition is special and so are you.

THREE

SENSUALITY, NOT SEXUALITY

There is a kind of cosmic joy in sensuality.
— *Jean Giono*

Gentry de Paris glided on gossamer through the doors of Café de Flore. In a deep-olive wool dress coat collared with faux fur and nipped at the waist, and with scarlet lipstick, her long black hair swept to the side à la Veronica Lake, she looked every inch a burlesque diva — which she was.

She really knew how to make an entrance. By the time Gentry reached my table, she had left bold stares and furtive glances in her wake. A waiter in a crisp white shirt and black vest swiftly appeared with two glasses of champagne. "From Monsieur," he said, acknowledging a man several tables over. "*Merci*," whispered Gentry toward the man, who nodded in return. I said *merci*, too, but Monsieur didn't notice.

"How do you do it?" I asked her.

"Intrigue and elegance, darling," she said. "Imagination does the rest."

I had met Gentry on the lingerie circuit. She was born Gentry Lane in Hollywood, California, and after bathing in the effervescence of the City of Light she refashioned herself as Gentry de Paris, femme fatale and lingerie designer. Gentry had always loved to sew, which was one of the reasons she became a designer. (Another was her impeccable taste.) The fashion elite of Paris dressed in her cashmere and silk designs. When she discovered that she liked wearing the pieces in her collection more than she liked making them, she reinvented herself once again as a burlesque dancer.

I had just seen her show, the *Gentry de Paris Revue with Dita Von Teese*, at the Casino de Paris. In it, she descended on a star as if from heaven while Dita frolicked in a gigantic martini glass of water. I wasn't the only one in the front row who got a little wet.

At the café, Gentry told me that she had recently opened the École Supérieure de Burlesque, the Elite School of Burlesque. I signed up immediately. I, too, wanted to learn the art of seduction. Christian and I now had five children and lived in a charming village south of Paris, and my days were filled with the quotidian — nannies, school-runs, laundry, groceries, and operating a small business. Survival was the name of the game, not seduction.

Seduction is an important word in the business of lingerie. Since I was a "lingerie professional," according to the box I ticked to register for trade shows and press events, I felt a certain responsibility to understand the full scope of its meaning. There is a difference between knowing. And *knowing*.

It is one of those words that is used a lot but never really explained. Asking about the particulars of seduction is like asking a magician, "How do you do it?" Answers are in the form of hitched smiles and obscure riddles instead of concrete tips and truths. At least, that's what it seemed to me.

On a Thursday night, twenty of us showed up to learn "Ten Ways To Remove Your Gloves." The classroom was in Gentry's Haussmann-style apartment behind the famous Galeries Lafayette. It had high molded ceilings, parquet flooring, and clothing racks brimming with sequins and boas.

Gentry greeted us wearing elbow-length satin gloves and a scarlet-red corset that matched the shade of her lipstick. She turned down the lights and turned up the music. Ella Fitzgerald singing Cole Porter's "Too Darn Hot." Stepping in front of a large gilded mirror that framed her and gave us a view from behind, she stood there, statuesque. With her forearm uplifted and palm facing her, she raised her chin, gripped the tip of her gloved index finger between her teeth, paused, and tugged gently. We were breathless, frozen in her gaze. While Lady Ella rhapsodized about the heat, Gentry shifted her hips and wriggled the rest of her fingers free. One. By. One. With a mischievous wink, she dangled her glove. With a slight shrug, she tossed it. As the glove floated to its fate, she turned on her heels and walked away.

We were dazzled.

"Whether you're taking out the garbage or taking off your

gloves, it's always about the tease," explained Gentry. "To frame a moment, you must slow it down and tease out the emotion."

Emotion. I hadn't thought about seduction like that before. Just as the Grinch finally realized that Christmas was about more than getting presents, I realized that maybe there was more to the art of seduction than getting naked. Gentry made it all look so carefree and fun. I wanted to have fun, too.

There are three *S* words that recur frequently when talking about lingerie. I think of them as the *S* triumvirate: seduction, sexuality, and sensuality. At first glance, they seem simple and straightforward — until you find yourself slipping and sliding down their sinuous curves. It is essential to feel comfortable and at ease with these words in order to appreciate the full potential and richness of lingerie.

SEDUCTION There is nothing ambiguous in the origin and meaning of *seduce*, which comes from the Latin *seducere*, meaning to lead away and astray with sexual motivations. In France, seduction is a game — not a competition — and having fun is more important than winning. Played both in private and in public, seduction is more about the possibility than the promise of sex. Anytime. Anywhere. And that creates an interesting dynamic and tension between heightened anticipation and a *très* relaxed attitude about sex and lingerie.

In America, there is nothing relaxed about the subject of sex, and there's nothing fun in the language of lingerie. Its marketing lexicon consists only of *sexy*, *hot*, and *sale*. The purpose and promise is clear. Lingerie = Sex. It's a faulty argument, though, when you consider what all women eventually learn: if sex is all that you're after, you don't need lingerie to get it. The truth is that Lingerie ≠ Sex. Sure, sex might be *better* with lingerie, but the same can be said of champagne.

SEXUALITY *Sexuality* would be nowhere without its overworked first cousin, *sexy*. Served up with a pout or a pucker, *sexy* is used to push everything from cars and appliances to fashion and food. Sex sells. I get it. But with lingerie there seems to be some consumer confusion in the marketplace. Who is the customer? (Hint: it's a she, not a he.) While men might enjoy a supporting role, women are the target audience, a detail too often neglected in advertising campaigns. Over the years, *sexy* has picked up a collective meaning, one that mirrors a male fantasy rather than reflecting our own. Women aren't asked; we are told what *sexy* means — and we buy into it hook, line, and sinker. *Romance* becomes a euphemism for sex, with flowers, music, and lingerie serving as stage props rather than acting as independent sources of pleasure and delight.

The success of lingerie chains and their ability to merchandize romance — and romanticize merchandise — is a telling example of the American lingerie narrative and message. Women wear lingerie to be sexy because they think that's what men want. The celebrated Victoria's Secret Fashion Show, which is broadcast on a major network and watched by millions around the world, is a testament to that. Angels and dreams sounds pretty heavenly — if you're a man. But these Vegas-destined angels aren't showing up in women's dreams; instead, they're giving us nightmares. The show leaves us feeling ashamed and inadequate instead of appreciating the glorious creatures that we are. Very few women will ever look like a Victoria's Secret angel — even if they wanted to — no matter how many "sexy," "hot," "sale" items they buy.

You might remember the iconic "Hello Boys" Wonderbra ad that was launched in the early nineties by Playtex, with busty Eva Herzigova staring down at her own breasts. Slogans for the campaign included, "Look me in the eyes ... I said the *eyes*"; "Do you notice anything about me?"; and "Plan to run into your ex." The global success of the ads created cleavage controversy but didn't stop women from flocking to buy the bra. Perhaps they hoped to defy gravity in exchange for some attention.

Consider, too, the lingerie shower tradition of frills, giggles, and champagne for the bride-to-be. I remember my lingerie shower. I received a lot of lacy-racy fashions and accessories that I believed would somehow transform me into a vixen *just by wearing them*. Women think of lingerie as a tested and approved method of seduction, and maybe even a guarantee of love. Advertising confirms it. While Victoria's Secret can be credited with making lingerie mainstream, at some level the conversation about lingerie has to be intimate and personal, and there doesn't seem to be anywhere to talk about that.

SENSUALITY In France the lingerie industry developed from a tradition of independent seamstresses and corset-makers. French girls grow up in a culture that fosters intimate settings for intimate conversations that include the sartorial accoutrements to seduction. As a result, French women wear lingerie for themselves. They don't need lingerie showers. Ask any French woman why she wears lingerie. She'll answer, *Pour moi, bien sûr*. For me, of course. Push the question further, as I have many times, and ask if she's hoping to have sex. She'll respond with amusement, *Peut-être; on va voir*. Maybe; we'll see. For her, sex is a detail — a detail that *she* will decide and manage. It is not the overriding objective.

At the same time that Eva Herzigova was causing traffic accidents, the French brand Aubade launched its triumphant "Lessons in Seduction" marketing campaign of exquisite black-and-white photos that were full of innuendo and accompanied by a playful, teasing "lesson." The campaign continues to create a sensation today, twenty-five years and more than one hundred and sixty lessons later. That's a lot of seduction. Even the one hundred sex positions in the *Kama Sutra* pale by comparison.

What's really going on in these photos? Each one shows a woman in various states of undress. The artistry of the photo captures the aura of a feminine essence. The body language and pose show a confident, relaxed woman. There is a quiet certainty in her demeanour. She's not looking for approval, nor does she need it. She has our attention and she knows it. For that reason alone, the photos are intensely provocative. Aside from the shadows in the curve of a breast or derrière, the content is very PG-rated — no gratuitous flash of flesh. The viewer never even sees the woman's face, but we don't need to see her facial expression to know what she means.

Each advertisement successfully creates intrigue, evokes emotion — and provokes desire.

Lesson No. 126 shows a woman standing with her back to us and wearing a small lacy black panty and black elbow-length gloves. The slogan reads, *Ne pas laisser d'empreintes*, don't leave any fingerprints. Lesson No. 55 shows a woman standing in a black lace camisole and panty. The slogan reads, *Créer de nouveaux frissons*, create new sensations. Lesson No. 39 shows a woman sitting in a demure white lace bra and panty and lace stockings. The slogan reads, *puis l'allonger sur le divan*, then lie down on the sofa.

The message is subtle but crystal clear: seduction is about sensuality, not sexuality. From design to marketing, the French understand the very fine line between elegant provocation and vulgarity, and dance on that line with grace.

Even in a culture celebrated for romance and envied for their *cinq à sept* — that time between 5 and 7 p.m. when one might be, shall we say, hard to track down — there are many more reasons to wear lingerie than just for your husband, boyfriend, or affair. Lingerie isn't a prerequisite for sex. Lingerie has a greater purpose.

I polled a dozen French lingerie designers to find out what words they like to use to describe lingerie, and not a single one said *sexy*. Their language was much more expressive: *subtle, elegant, surprising, feminine, pleasurable, poetic, refined, romantic, natural, timeless, liberating* — and the most highly cited, *sensual*.

There is something soft and inviting about the word *sensuality*, but what does it mean? More important, does one have to acquire it or are we born with it?

It is no surprise that the word *sensuality* pertains to the five senses, with its origins from Late Latin, *sensualitas*, meaning "capacity for sensation," and from Latin, *sensus*, suggesting perception, feeling, meaning.

A sensation is a physical feeling. It is how your body reacts when one of the senses is triggered. Think of words like: *soft, tender, fluttery, dizzy, breathless, prickly, itchy, tight, sweaty, calm, light, warm, smooth.* The list is endless. Sensuality is the chance to revel in all the fun sensations. Lingerie transforms the routine of getting dressed from a limited linear experience to an enriched sensorial one that has a ripple effect throughout the day. Both take the same amount of time, but dressing with intention adds layers and dimensions.

What sensations do you identify with lingerie? Pick out your favourite bra and panty. Put them on. How do you feel? Good? Great! But what does *good* mean? Trust your body. Listen to it. What do you notice? A lightness? Heaviness? The same way learning to pair foods enhances enjoyment, learning to pair textures provides endless sensations and delights. Try wearing lace panties underneath jeans, a silk bra beneath a wool sweater, or a cotton bodysuit under a flouncy dress. Every combination has something different and unique to offer. The very act of paying attention to your lingerie — and sensations — changes your experience.

Sensuality is the beauty and mystery that lies in the space between modesty and provocation. It is entirely personal. There are no rules, no guidelines, just an invitation. Start making your lingerie decisions based on their tactile potential and the ability to provoke sensations and inspire feelings and emotion. Wearing lingerie is a chance to experience the shiver and pleasure of sensuality.

With or *sans* sex.

BEHIND THE SEAMS

THE ART OF FRENCH LINGERIE

A look at the skilled craftsmanship that makes French lingerie so exceptional

FOUR

A HERITAGE

Real elegance is everywhere,
especially in the things that don't show.
— Christian Dior

I chose an 1890 golden-olive silk corset trimmed with black lace and an undulating stripe of pink ribbon. What better way to understand the history of lingerie than to time travel back to the nineteenth century, laced up in one of the era's most beautiful corsets? And with none other than Ghislaine Rayer, the owner of Nuits de Satin and the largest private collection of historic lingerie in the world, as your tour guide. Her lavishly decorated showroom in Garches, an exclusive suburb of Paris, has more than 5,000 pieces from between 1770 and 1990, and is larger than most textile museums.

Lacing me up turned out to be a complicated affair, and a misnomer as well. I had expected a bunch of fussy little satin strings, but the actual "laces" had serious work to do, and were constructed accordingly. Though dyed the same colour as the golden-olive silk, the ties were more like flat cotton shoelaces. The thinner you want your waist to look, the harder someone has to tug.

That's right. Putting on a corset requires a designated tugger.

"You should have stopped eating a week ago," teased Ghislaine as she tightened the reins behind me — pulling here, adjusting there — until all thirty-eight whalebone stays closed in around me.

Once thoroughly yanked and tucked, I rested my hands on my hips, around my now very pronounced waist.

"Divine," cooed Ghislaine. Indeed. Keenly aware of my body, I discerned a newfound grace and carriage.

"What a shame that women were made to believe that beautiful lingerie was worn only to please your partner," said Ghislaine, observing my delighted reaction to my appearance. "I think the feminists made a mistake; when women stopped wearing beautiful lingerie to seduce they didn't realize they were also depriving themselves of a personal pleasure."

Perhaps during all this time of emancipation and feminism, we tried so hard for our voices to be heard that we became numbed to the inherent pleasure and joy of our bodies. Ghislaine certainly thought so. "Pretty lingerie is elemental to one's well-being and esteem. It's an essential part of our being."

Ghislaine's passion for lingerie began at age thirteen, when she read Emile Zola's *Au Bonheur des Dames*, *The Ladies' Paradise*. The novel is set in the late nineteenth century during the rise of department stores, which radically transformed fashion and shopping habits. Seduced by Zola's descriptions of lingerie fabrics, Ghislaine longed to *"connaître cette sensation de toucher,"* know that feeling of touch. The very first piece she picked up was a corset that had been worn by the lead actress in *Nana*, the movie made from the eponymous book penned by Zola about a young girl's rise from street prostitute to high-class courtesan. Women's stories, personal lives, daily habits, hopes, and dreams could all be deciphered and retold through the most intimate of garments.

The word *corset* is derived from the Latin *corpus*, meaning "body." Before the bra, girdles, personal trainers, fad diets, and cosmetic surgery, a woman reshaped her body by way of whalebones, padding, hoops, and lacing. Busts, waists, and bottoms were accentuated or minimized depending on what was in vogue. Vital organs were squished by corsets laced up so tightly that women could barely bend at the waist, let alone breathe. Imagine your waist cinched down to a mere forty-six-centimetre diameter—the size of a medium pizza!

Corsets first appeared in Europe in the early sixteenth century and were made from stiff fabric and materials that later included wood, steel, cane, or boning sewn into the seams or linings for even more rigidity. By the early nineteenth century, the corset industry was booming, with France leading the way. Everyone wore a corset. Rich or poor, courtesan or nursing mother, there was an appropriate corset for the occasion: basic beige corsets stripped of any adornment for those who could only afford the minimum, and luxurious detailed corsets for upper-class clientele.

The finest corsets were made in Paris, handcrafted using stunning silks, laces, and intricate flossing (decorative embroidery) for the more demanding clients. Whalebone stays — elongated strips of bone inserted into the fabric — provided strength, shape, and flexibility. Busks, the hook-and-eye closures attached to long metal strips down the front, helped flatten the stomach and straighten the posture.

"Respectable" women wore elaborately detailed corsets in muted colours while elaborately detailed corsets in vibrant colours were reserved for courtesans. Wealthy *fureurs de mode*, fashion addicts, throughout the world coveted the splendour and luxury of a *corset de Paris*.

"Refinement was an art," explained Ghislaine. "Well-dressed women of those days were layered like an onion." Getting dressed in the morning took time. Underneath the corset, next to the skin, women wore a cotton chemise. After all, it was an era before regular bathing and one-hour dry cleaning. The chemise helped protect the corset from dirt, stains, and odours, as did the *cache-corset*, a light cotton top that women wore to cover the corset.

And that was only the top of the body. The bottom half was covered with an abundance of *jupons* — petticoats of various thickness and quality that indicated a woman's social status:

more petticoats, more status. "The French expression *frou-frou* that now describes lingerie frills actually comes from the rustling sounds made by those petticoat layers of silk, tulle, and cotton as they swished together: *froufroufroufroufroufrou*," Ghislaine explained.

❧

Lingerie as we know it originated in the mid-nineteenth century when Emperor Napoleon III ushered in an era of the *grande bourgeoisie*, or upper class, where wealth was on display. Men with aristocratic titles weren't necessarily the ones making all the money, and those who were successful were now entitled to a few aristocratic perks — like having both a wife and a mistress. Those perks didn't come cheap. Wives and mistresses were expected to dress and undress in layers of attractive clothing. Distinction and style reigned.

But it was several decades later, during the *belle époque*, meaning "beautiful era," when the most refined corsets were produced. This magnificent period in France began in the late nineteenth century and lasted until World War I. Characterized by tremendous innovation in the arts and sciences, the *belle époque* was also a time of prosperity, thanks to the continued effects of the Industrial Revolution that made raw materials easier to import and finished products easier to export.

In 1869, visionary businessman Aristide Boucicault changed the face of commerce forever when he opened the doors to Le Bon Marché, one of the first department stores in the world. The store organized its wares in sections that overflowed with merchandise. Boucicault fixed prices, introduced exchanges and refunds, drove sales through advertising, and targeted customers directly by mailing out six million fashion catalogues, each one containing actual fabric swatches.

What did this mean for lingerie? Women could browse a catalogue or in person. They no longer needed a personal seamstress to handcraft their undergarments. Shopping became a social activity where different classes mingled and thrived. Women could shop all day unescorted, or they could leave their husbands in a reading room and their children in an activity area. At its peak, Le Bon Marché welcomed more than 15,000 customers a day.

As the nineteenth century progressed, so did the push for women's emancipation and the desire to take a deep breath without a piece of whalebone getting in the way. Change was in the air as corset-makers on both sides of the Atlantic struggled to find a way to cut the corset in half. It was like trying to split the atom. Some filed patents for "breast supporters," some made prototypes, and some even sold a few. But only one managed to commercialize her idea with any success.

And that someone was corset-maker Herminie Cadolle.

Herminie Cadolle unveiled her new creation: the *corselet-gorge*, a two-piece corset, during the 1889 World's Fair in Paris, which celebrated the one-hundredth anniversary of the storming of the Bastille and the inauguration of Gustave Eiffel's skyline-changing tower.

The *corselet-gorge* caught on, and with a resounding collective gasp, women busted out of the corset once and for all. Over the years, the *corselet-gorge* would undergo many modifications and become known as a *soutien-gorge*, which literally translates to "throat support." It was the beginning of the modern bra.

Between the advent of the bra and women taking more active roles in public and private life, there was less of a need for the corsets and the exaggerated curves of the *belle époque*. By World War I, they were obsolete. What we think of today as lingerie — bra + panty + garter — began in the 1920s, when the feminine silhouette turned slender and boyish. No curves, no restrictions, no onion layers. Bandeau bras flattened breasts, and more rigid fabrics held in larger busts. Flappers wore loose-fitting one-piece cami-knickers (a camisole and tap pant all rolled into one) to maintain dignity while doing the Charleston.

By the 1930s, the trend for flat had flattened. Undergarments shaped up into defined cups as Warner's introduced the Alphabet Bra — a universal A through D sizing system to standardize cup sizes.

Beyond societal changes, engineering innovations have always been a driving influence on the architecture of lingerie. Market demand leads to innovation and innovation leads to more freedom.

The invention of nylon in 1938, for example, made all lingerie more affordable. With improved manufacturing methods and the decrease in price, lingerie was no longer a luxury item reserved for the elite.

In particular, nylon totally revolutionized stockings. Women lined up to buy an estimated sixty-four million pairs of sheer nylon stockings the first year they appeared on the market. Rayon had already existed as an alternative to more expensive silk, but nylon boasted a longer list of superlative qualities: strength, resilience, easy to wash, inexpensive. And it was a dream to dye. Colours began to diversify, allowing for brilliant new shades. Nylon also helped popularize the colour black, which had previously been problematic to set due to dye-fixing problems.

Nylon wasn't the only tech advancement that had a big impact on this industry. Imagine lingerie today without stretch. Lastex, for example, was an early stretch yarn developed in the 1930s that gave elastic properties to the fabrics with which it was blended. Lastex made a big splash in the swimsuit market, which had previously been dominated by wool — a heavy and hot fabric when dry and a sodden mass when wet. Strong and light, Lastex fabrics smoothed and flattered women's bodies instead of distorting them, a trait that also helped launch girdles and other foundation garments.

Along the way, fashion changed with the culture, and vice versa. In the fifties, style evoked structure and glamour. Lingerie was "the quintessence of femininity," according to Ghislaine, who considers this decade — without a doubt — the most beautiful period in lingerie history, one that transcended fashion and crossed continents. While the *belle époque* was indeed, beautiful, the rise of Dior's New Look heralded a new era and celebrated a silhouette with slim waist, graceful hips, narrow shoulders, and defined breasts. Hourglass figures and corsets made a comeback.

Now, it's one thing to imagine an hourglass figure, but it's another to actually shape one. Such a silhouette wouldn't have been possible without the expertise and *savoir faire* of corset-makers. One of those corset-makers was Marie-Rose Lebigot whose motto, "the figure makes the woman, the waist makes the figure, the corset makes the waist," inspired her work with couturier Marcel Rochas to create the *guêpière*, or basque, an all-in-one garment that combined bustier, corset, short skirt, and garter belt. While form-fitting, the *guêpière* was less restrictive than a corset, but still delivered on its promise of a *taille de guêpe*, wasp waist.

Throughout the fifties, the fusion of technology and fashion continued to create the perfect form. Metal underwire and fittings gave the bra of that era a more struc-tured and rigid look. Cups were tapered and stiffened to torpedo dimensions. Models wore tight sweaters in pin-up posters and those posters got pinned up, which pro-moted and maintained the postwar ideal of a full and pointed bust. And in the late 1950s, Dupont invented a miracle stretch fibre that is recognized more by its brand name — Lycra — than by its generic names: elastane in Europe and spandex in North America. It reshaped just about everything. The women of the sixties, however, rejected anything structured and strove for comfort and freedom of expression. Many opted not to wear a bra at all, and French lingerie brands floundered, resulting in many bankruptcies.

Pants became the rage in the 1970s as women's emanci-pation continued, and simplified bras with less structure also prevailed. For a new generation of women, freedom was worn as unisex, and nudity was celebrated on the beach and through light, transparent fabrics that made bras and panties seemingly invisible. By the end of the decade, however, women began to once again look at lingerie with an eye toward the game of seduction.

In the eighties, the irreverent, ultra-feminine French designer Chantal Thomass made seduction fashionable again. Black became more mainstream. Women wore their LBB (Little Black Bra) underneath their LBD (Little Black Dress). Gradually, lingerie styles began to blur the threshold of what is considered erotic. The decade closed with the one-hundredth anniversary of the bra.

A sense of calm returned in the nineties, along with a "less is more" attitude that countered the extravagance of the eighties. Microfibre and molded cups accentuated natural curves and teased a sense of false modesty.

Today, there is So. Much. Choice. A quick survey of major retailers reveals a dizzying number of lingerie categories: sporty, sexy, maternity, natural, classic, and designer. There is something for every personality and every occasion and season, and marketing plans to keep customers coming back.

To the women who were accustomed to corsets, the bra represented freedom, and for the early feminist movement, the bra symbolized oppression. Now the bra is the ultimate sensual purchase. Freedom, oppression, sensuality; it's all so confusing. For decades, we've been tightening and loosening our undergarments, and shaping and reshaping our bodies. Lingerie has played a defining role in a woman's sense of identity and femininity, and undergarments have evolved over time, blending function and aesthetics.

Perhaps the challenge now, in the twenty-first century,

is to feel so at ease in our bodies that our lingerie is simply a natural extension and expression of who we are, regardless of cultural expectations and current fashions. As we write the next chapters of lingerie history together, let's focus on what lingerie means to each one of us, individually, instead of to a collective group of gender-related people. Perhaps the ultimate freedom of movement now is the freedom to just *be*.

AN ILLUSTRATED HISTORY OF THE BRA

Bra.

It's a small name for a small article of clothing. Yet, the bra plays a huge role in our wardrobe, and in our lives. Most of the time we don't give our bra a second thought — except that we expect it to be right there, ready for duty, day after day after day: to hold us up, hold us in, make our clothes look good, and make us feel sexy.

Today's bra as we know it — two cups, two straps, and a band — is the result of decades of design and technological innovation. The illustration on the next page highlights some of the most important design and technological innovations in the evolution of the bra.

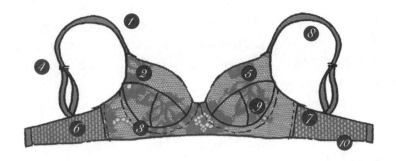

1. **1889** — French corset-maker Herminie Cadolle presented a *corselet-gorge* (bra) at the World's Fair in Paris. Breasts are no longer supported from underneath, but from above, by straps.

2. **1889** — Rayon, the first manufactured fibre, is invented. It is not used by lingerie manufacturers until the 1920s, when it is added for softness and smoothness.

3. **1920S** — Underwire is added to bra cups for more shaping and support, but is not popularized until the 1950s.

4. **1930S** — The sliding metal ring and other bra components appeared to help adjust straps for a better fit.

5. **1937** — Warner's introduced cup sizing from A to D.

6. **1938** — Dupont invented nylon, which revolutionized lingerie.

7. **1958** — Dupont invented elastane (Lycra). When blended, this fibre can stretch any fabric seven times its original length.

8. **1962** — Elastic, adjustable straps are invented.

9. **1982** — Stretch lace is created by incorporating Lycra in traditional designs.

10. **1984** — Microfibre is used for the first time in lingerie, adding unprecedented softness and lightness.

FIVE

ANATOMY OF A BRA

*It is not sufficient to see and to know the beauty of
a work. We must feel and be affected by it.*
—Voltaire

The French have a lovely expression, *décolleté de rêve*. It means "neckline of dreams" or "a beautiful neckline." When was the last time you put on a bra and saw the neckline of your dreams?

If only shopping for a bra were as simple as shopping for shoes. You feel a rush of excitement when you see the right pair. The thrill mounts as you pull them from their nest of tissue paper and a salesperson slips them onto your feet. You are Cinderella. Your confidence swells as you sashay to the mirror and confirm what you already know: the shoes make you look amazing. You *are* amazing! You leave the store euphoric, and you didn't have to undress in front of a stranger.

Now let's go bra shopping.

Dismayed by the sad, stretched, greying specimens in your drawer, you trudge off to a department store. You take the escalator to a section called Intimate Apparel, which sounds like a dispensary for maxi pads. Scanning the endless rows of bras whose distinctions escape you, you begin to feel dizzy from the jargon: Deep U Plunge, Extreme V, Miracle Lift, 3D Contour. You grab a simple ivory bra off the rack and ask for it in a 36B, the size you think you are, or the size that you used to be, anyway.

As you are surveying yourself dispiritedly in the mirror of a badly lit dressing room, a saleswoman yanks the curtain aside and gives your body a critical eye: "Too much back fat," she says.

Just what you wanted to hear.

You could smack her, but she's right. Clumps of flesh bulge between the bra strap and your shoulder blades. "I'll bring you the sister size," she says, whatever that means.

The so-called sister size gapes at the sides. The saleswoman looks displeased. She returns again with a medley of bras dangling from her arm like spaghetti. You smile gamely.

The fluorescent lights are giving you a headache, and you look like you've put on five pounds just standing there.

An hour later, your breasts are cradled in a 32E, a size that cannot possibly exist. "It fits perfectly!" confirms the saleswoman. Maybe, but the bra looks like it belonged to your Aunt Ethel. You go home exhausted and toss your newest acquisition, along with your self-esteem, into a drawer of dashed lingerie dreams.

What is it about finding the right bra that causes so much distress? No other article of clothing in our wardrobe plays such an important role (or has such power to influence our relationships!). A bra affects our posture, mood, and, ultimately, the shape of everything else we wear; yet we are rarely satisfied with our selection. The right bra must do more than lift and shape, but we can't always get what we want. We don't always get what we need, either.

The result? Too many unwanted, unworn bras, and a phobia about ever getting it right.

You don't have to be a cobbler to understand the basic components of a shoe. If the heel is too high, you teeter. If the toe is too narrow, it pinches.

The bra remains enigmatic. Most women think their bra fits when it doesn't, and don't know what to look for so that it will.

You may be surprised to learn that the bra is actually an engineering masterpiece composed of ten to forty pieces. The art of it lies in the designer's ability to put those pieces together in a way that makes you fall in love with your body.

Knowing the various pieces and understanding how a bra is constructed is the first step toward making better choices. If it doesn't look or feel the way you want, *the problem is the bra, not you.*

You'd expect nothing less from your shoes. If your shoes didn't fit or flatter your feet, you'd drop them on their sorry soles.

The following alphabetized list identifies the eight essential bra parts you should know. So, sit back. Relax. Go ahead — take your shoes off!

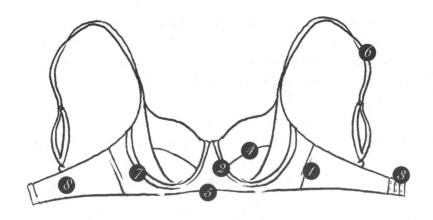

1. BAND

WHAT IS IT? What do you think actually holds your breasts up? (Hint: It's not the shoulder straps.) That's right, it's the band! The band size is the measurement taken around your chest, just under your breasts, and constitutes the number part of your bra size; for example, the 34 in 34A, 34B, 34C.

WHY IS IT IMPORTANT? The band anchors the cups and distributes the weight of your breasts. The band should lie horizontally across your back, forming a 90-degree angle with the base of your neck. It should feel taut, not tight.

ANYTHING ELSE I NEED TO KNOW? You'll know the band is doing its job if you raise and lower your arms and the band doesn't budge. If it slides up, it's too big. If you can't breathe, it's too small.

2. CENTRE GORE

WHAT IS IT? The centre gore (also referred to as the centre front) is what joins the cups in the middle.

WHY IS IT IMPORTANT? The centre gore anchors the overall structure of the bra. This small piece is one of the determining factors for fit. Check to see that the centre gore lies flat against your sternum. If it does, good. If it floats, you need to consider a different size.

ANYTHING ELSE I NEED TO KNOW? The centre gore varies in shape and size, depending on bra style. For example, the gore is shorter in a plunge bra and taller in a cup that gives more coverage. The gore can also complement different breast shapes and development. If your breasts are set closely together, it is likely that a style with a narrow gore would fit best. If your breasts are set farther apart, a wider gore is recommended.

3. CLOSURE

WHAT IS IT? Most bras do up in the back with a hook-and-eye closure that is attached to the band. This is the most popular style, although there are others.

WHY IS IT IMPORTANT? The band should feel snug, but over time it will stretch. The hook-and-eye closure allows you to adjust and tighten to ensure that your band stays firmly in place.

ANYTHING ELSE I NEED TO KNOW? When trying on a bra for the first time, fasten it on the loosest setting so that you can tighten it over time. On the side that touches your skin, look for a brushed back for a softer feel. Other closures, such as a front clasp, are also fine, but offer fewer options for adjustment.

4. CUP

WHAT IS IT? The cup is the part of the bra that cradles, supports, and shapes the breast. The cup is the letter part of the bra size; for example, the B in 32B, 34B, 36B.

WHY IS IT IMPORTANT? Different cup styles create different bust lines. Depending on the design, the cup can also increase or minimize volume to achieve a certain look.

ANYTHING ELSE I NEED TO KNOW? Yes, and this next piece of information makes the idea that the earth is flat sound plausible: Even though the cup is represented by the letter in the bra size — the B of a 32B — guess what? There is no such thing as a standard B-cup size.

That's right, a universal B cup does not exist. Crazy, I know! It causes confusion for everyone. Why would an industry do that? Wouldn't it make more sense to have a simple sizing system? Sure, but no centralized Department of Bra Sizing has been set up to regulate policy, and that isn't about to change any time soon. As the saying goes, if you can't beat 'em, join 'em, so here's what you need to know: The cup size is actually the difference between the measurement taken from around your chest over the fullest part of your breasts, and the measurement from around your chest underneath your breasts. This number indicates the distance in inches that your breasts project from your body, which corresponds to a cup size. Each cup size varies by one inch:

A-cup projects breasts 1 inch

B-cup projects breasts 2 inches

C-cup projects breasts 3 inches

D-cup projects breasts 4 inches

To achieve this projection, the band size must alter, which is the theory behind "sister sizes." A sister size refers to the same volume, or cup size, that can be found in a different bra size. For example, a 32B has the same cup size as 34A. A 36C has the same cup size as a 34D. Same volume, different band length.

Are you feeling faint? It's a lot to swallow, I know. It's a good thing you don't have to memorize this. The following chart is a handy reference that outlines the different sister sizes. All sizes running diagonally to the right in the same colour have the same cup size. It's confusing at first, but once you understand the chart, you'll know what to do when a bra doesn't feel right.

Sister Sizes

30A	30B	30C	30D	30E	30F	30G	30H	30I
32A	32B	32C	32D	32E	32F	32G	32H	32I
34A	34B	34C	34D	34E	34F	34G	34H	34I
36A	36B	36C	36D	36E	36F	36G	36H	36I
38A	38B	38C	38D	38E	38F	38G	38H	38I
40A	40B	40C	40D	40E	40F	40G	40H	40I
42A	42B	42C	42D	42E	42F	42G	42H	42I
44A	44B	44C	44D	44E	44F	44G	44H	44I

5. FRAME (CRADLE)

WHAT IS IT? The frame of the bra is a separate piece of fabric in which the cups sit.

WHY IS IT IMPORTANT? It anchors the cups and provides optimal support.

ANYTHING ELSE I NEED TO KNOW? Not all bras are designed with a frame; cups can join directly at the centre gore. But if you need more support, a bra with a frame is a good solution.

6. STRAP

WHAT IS IT? The bra strap is attached at one end to the top of the cup, and at the other end to the back band. It likely includes a ring and slider to make easy adjustments.

WHY IS IT IMPORTANT? The bra strap fixes the cup and band in the correct position, but it should not be carrying the weight of the breasts. (You remember, right? It's the *band* that holds your breasts aloft.)

A strap made with good quality elastic stays in place and doesn't fall off your shoulders. The elastic needs to be able to stretch. Even more important, all elastic needs good "recovery," or the ability to return to its original shape. Test the stretch: Pull the elastic and release. Flimsy elastic will be too easy to stretch and will not recover properly, while a firm elastic will be more difficult to stretch and recover 100 percent.

ANYTHING ELSE I NEED TO KNOW? Bra straps should be only partly elastic. This is why you often see a decorative motif, such as a flower bud or rosette, positioned at the apex (the part of the bra where the cup joins the strap) to block and minimize stretch.

7. UNDERWIRE

WHAT IS IT? Underwire is the piece of metal or plastic, gently curved, like a smile, that is sewn into the bottom of the bra cup.

WHY IS IT IMPORTANT? Bras that have underwire fit and shape better than bras without. The underwire should completely cradle the breasts and lie flat underneath the breast tissue. If it doesn't, it's likely that the cups are too small.

ANYTHING ELSE I NEED TO KNOW? Despite lingering misgivings by some, there is no conclusive medical evidence that any harm or health hazard is caused by wearing underwire. However, it is logical (and more comfortable!) to make sure that the underwire in your bra is as effective as possible. Casings with a plush side next to the skin are more comfortable and a sign of a better quality bra. They can either be tubular or flat. Underwire in flat casings position the cup better and don't roll around.

8. WING

WHAT IS IT? The wing is the section of the band between the cups and the closure.

WHY IS IT IMPORTANT? The wings wrap around your back to pull the bra into position.

ANYTHING ELSE I NEED TO KNOW? Check for elasticity in the fabric the same way you did for your bra straps. This part of the bra also needs a firm stretch.

~

I've explained all the parts — which is kind of like telling you that the foot bone's connected to the leg bone and the leg bone's connected to the knee bone. But how do all these parts make a sensual whole? Determined to find out, I bought two bras, one of better quality than the other — and a seam ripper.

I can't sew, but I can un-sew. My mission? Take apart each bra — stitch by stitch — to discover its secrets.

First, the one of poorer quality: a padded cobalt-blue nylon bra trimmed with a lace of similar colour and a small silver heart in the centre gore. At first glance, it looked pretty. I turned the bra over in my hands and contemplated where to make the first incision. I went straight for the heart, hooked the seam ripper, and yanked. Next, I began unstitching the casing that holds the underwire, which exposed the ragged edges of the padding. The loosely sewn lace pulled off easily. Like a house of cards, the bra fell apart. I left the back closure attached to the band, but noticed that the hooks were covered in white enamel and were already chipped, like a bad manicure. Tattered fabric pieces and frayed thread lay in front of me — everything almost the same colour, but not quite.

The well-made bra was black, padded, and covered in lace

with scalloped edges floating as overlay on the cup. The top half of the bra strap was made with two spaghetti straps covered in black satin. An embroidered daisy cutout covered the seam between the straps and the cups. Another daisy sparkled with a Swarovski crystal in the centre gore. Black lace covered the band, extending to the black back closure with gold-coloured hooks. The first cut is the deepest, and I didn't want to make it.

The stitching was hard to see. I gripped the casing with one hand and the bra cup with the other and pulled. Nothing. My second attempt yielded a slight give. On the third I succeeded in finding the line of stitching, and slid the seam ripper underneath. After a series of short and quick thrusts the thread broke and I worked my way down the seam. Grip. Pull. Hook. Snip. Repeat. The covered padding peeled back to reveal black-covered foam and layers of saturated black that would have remained invisible had I not exposed them. The growing pile of thread had a slight shimmer and, although wrinkled, wasn't frayed. Each one of the separated components was as elegant on its own as when it had been part of a greater whole.

Hours later (undoing takes time!), I'd made a mess and found my answer. Sensuality lies in the nuances and details: invisible stitching, finished seams, precise colour matching, and no stray threads or unmatched pieces. The quality of the well-made bra reverberated throughout, right down to the coated underwire that no one ever sees.

The process of taking apart those two bras gave me an insight into how fine lingerie is deliberately designed to *éveiller les sens*, awaken the senses. If you have a bra that you no longer wear and are curious, try this exercise yourself. The process will paradoxically demystify the bra as a series of components and induce delight and enchantment.

Good lingerie designers do more than just assemble parts. They create a work of art.

The same way master chefs use a list of ingredients and the best knives to craft a memorable meal, lingerie designers transform fabric using needle and thread and the right fabrics to create a composition that triggers emotion — and, of course, that fits and shapes.

That's a lot to ask from a bra. And that's why there are many different bra styles to provide nuanced shaping and sculpting.

BRA STYLES

BALCONNETTE: The expression *Il y a du monde au balcon,* everyone is on the balcony, refers to the privileged view from the balcony at the opera of the bosoms below. *Balconnette* means "shelf," or "balcony," and this bra style covers only the lower part of the breast to lift and enhance, giving a straight bust line. It is well-suited for smaller busts. Straps are attached to the sides of the cups.

DEMI OR HALF CUP: Referred to as *corbeille* in French, this form is ideal for larger breasts. Covering half to three-quarters of the breast, the cup is shaped to give a plump, upward-rounded curve while providing the necessary support. This bra enhances cleavage, giving a fuller bust line.

FULL CUP: This classic shape with deep cups provides full coverage and support. Underwire is almost always present in full-cup bras. This style is suitable for medium to very generous breasts.

MOLDED: This technique involves placing fabric on a mold and heating under high pressure to create a seamless, pre-formed cup. Molded cups are comfortable and give breasts a natural, smooth, and discreet shape under tight clothing.

PUSH-UP: Angled cups with padding push the breasts together, enhancing cleavage and creating an illusion of volume. Ideal for low necklines. Both small-busted and full-busted women can wear this style, but if your push-up lifts you off the ground, you might want to consider leaving more to the imagination.

PLUNGE: The French use the English word, too, so there is no escaping the vertigo. But if you insist on wearing *that* dress, you're going to need this bra. Ideal for the deepest of necklines, a plunge bra has a lower centre gore — the fabric between the cups — which increases cleavage while maintaining support. Wide-set straps expose neckline and cleavage.

SEAMED: Referred to as "cut and sew," these bras are made of two or three pieces that are sewn together, creating seams that are designed to lift, control, and shape. Follow the seam and you'll see the direction and how it is working to help shape your breast, whether pushing up with a vertical seam in the middle, achieving more roundness from a horizontal and curved seam, or coaxing your breasts forward with a line of stitching on the side. Often criticized for showing through clothing, seamed bras shouldn't be overlooked in favour of the molded T shirt bra, as smooth fabrics (such as stretchy lace) can be very discreet under clothing. These bras really do provide the best fit.

STRAPLESS: Because the band does most of the work in every style, this is actually the perfect solution for backless fashions. Look for at least a three-hook closure to ensure that the band is capable of doing its job. However, some styles are not as suitable. For instance, if you are large breasted and wear a full cup, a strapless bra might not be the best option for you because there are no straps to keep the cups in place. If you don't feel completely free to move, you may need to rethink your wardrobe choice.

SPORTS BRA: The more you move, the better you feel — unless your breasts are doing all the bouncing and swinging. The Research Group in Breast Health at the University of Portsmouth, England, has confirmed that wearing an adapted sports bra can cut down on vertical and horizontal breast motion up to 80 percent, which can reduce pain, sagging, and maybe some embarrassment. "Breathable" fabrics made from microfibres will wick away the moisture before it has a chance to absorb into your clothes, trap sweat, and cause skin irritations and discomfort.

Take the time to try these different styles and feel the difference. Which form or forms give you your own *décolleté de rêve*?

SIX

FEEL THE DIFFERENCE

*My mother was right: When you've got
nothing left, all you can do is get into silk
underwear and start reading Proust.*
— *Jane Birken*

Everyone knows that a good breakfast is important. For some it's a blissful moment; for others, breakfast is eaten in a fog and soaked in caffeine. The phrase "you are what you eat" offers a vivid reminder of the benefits of a healthy diet and the consequences of too many poor choices. We understand the importance of nourishing ourselves — both literally and figuratively. However, when it comes to clothing, "you are what you wear" refers more to the exterior — fashion and style — than to what lies underneath. Both the fibre in our breakfast and the fibre in our lingerie affect the well-being of our body and mind.

Take this little quiz. This morning you selected for your lingerie:

a) a T-shirt bra and organic cotton panty

b) a bra that scratches and a thong that's creeping up

c) a matching deep-purple silk bra and panty that cost more than your cellphone

d) a sports bra...it's laundry day

e) can't remember

Well-being and wellness aren't reserved for green smoothies and yoga retreats. Many women mistakenly believe that if they could change their bodies, they would feel better about themselves — more confident, attractive, elegant, sensual, or sexy. They see lingerie as a reward rather than a means to feeling good right now. But here's the lingerie paradox: by focusing on how you *feel* in your lingerie instead of how you *look*, you'll improve your body image...*without changing your body*.

Here's why.

Different fabrics evoke different sensations and feelings, and the right fabrics enhance your body, finding expression in the choreography of your movements — as your legs take you home from work, as your arms wrap around your best friend, as your knees bend to tie the laces on your child's shoes, as your hips shimmy and shake during Zumba class, and as your body presses into the contours of the one you love. Good lingerie moves with you.

There's more. You might think it makes no difference what

your lingerie is made of, but it does. It factors into how well the bra is made, how well it will hold up over time, whether it's good for the environment, and whether or how much it stretches or wicks moisture away from the body. Certain fabrics hold colour better. Others last longer. It is essential, as a good consumer, to understand the choices you have when choosing lingerie, and to be confident you have spent your money wisely.

Lingerie has the capacity to awaken, cradle, and soothe us. There is an invisible and sensitive layer between being naked and dressed that is often overlooked in the quest for lingerie that pushes up or out. If you feel nothing, you're missing out.

Stop. Breathe. Feel.

À fleur de peau is a popular name for lingerie boutiques in France. With the words flower (*fleur*) and skin (*peau*), I imagined it meant a bed of rose petals, until Madame Annabelle set me straight, again.

"It has nothing to do with flowers," said Madame Annabelle. "It means the surface of the skin."

"Ah, the epidermis," I said.

"Just on top," specified Madame Annabelle. "Think of *affleurer*, to touch lightly, or *effleurer*, to brush up against. *À fleur de peau* means just on the surface — the sensation of something very close, like the touch of a lover who makes you tremble."

Skin is our largest organ — the first touch screen ever! Consider the amazing science involved. Our skin keeps our insides from falling out, which is a really good thing, and it helps house the sensory receptors along with the dermis and subcutaneous fat. Can't remember what they are? Neither could I, so I brushed up on my grade ten biology.

A sensory receptor is a nerve with a special ending that picks ups signals of what's happening around us and sends this information to the brain for processing and interpretation. Like doormen, sensory receptors are always ready, 24/7. They also have cool names that make them sound as if they're buddies of Mozart: Merkel, Meissner, Ruffini, Krause, and Pacinian.

The receptors respond to different stimuli, such as touch, temperature, pressure, pain, and vibrations. Meanwhile, our experience of these sensations differs depending on whether the touch is active or passive.

Active touch is initiated and executed by you. Watch any creative person: designers at a fabric show, painters in their studios, or scrapbookers and knitters in their living rooms. They engage with their materials and they touch and manipulate. Much of their enjoyment comes from the hands-on creative process, not just the beauty of the end product.

Passive touch happens *to* you; for example, the feeling of someone caressing your cheek or how you perceive the comfort of a garment on your body. Certain sensory receptors only activate when they feel something being put on or taken off. The rest of the time, you might not be aware of any particular sensation unless a tag starts to rub, a piece of lace scratches, or an underwire digs in. Discomfort is picked up by another type of sensory receptor, which sends a message to the brain to determine if the discomfort is simply mild irritation or a greater threat.

Active touch and passive touch become particularly interesting when making lingerie choices. Tracing the outline of a lace motif or a piece of embroidery feels different than wearing it. In the first scenario, you are actively caressing the details with your fingers. In the second, you are feeling the passive touch of the reverse side of the bra or panty. Therefore, your perception and interpretation of comfort can be misleading; how and what you feel when you touch lingerie with your fingers isn't the same feeling you'll have when you're wearing it.

Fabric composition labels are growing more elaborate, while savvy marketing departments create captivating taglines and persuasive arguments designed to convince rather than explain. Here's a look at the fibres and the fabrics you wear closest to your body. Understanding the basics will help you recognize what to look for so you can select lingerie that will caress and *affleurer* your skin. Lingerie that offers joy, surprise, and comfort is dependent on fibres — the nutritional elements, so to speak — of good clothing.

AN ODE TO SILK

Lingerie is made from only a few fabrics and silk tops the feel-good list, so I'm going to give it special recognition before going through the rest. Soft and delicate, the sensation of silk transcends the divine. I am reminded of Stendhal's words when trying to describe its incomparable softness: "Pleasure is often spoiled by describing it." Nevertheless, the detailed story of silk is fascinating. (Spoiler alert: it ends badly for the silkworm.)

The Chinese were the first to discover and harness the magic of the industrious, short-lived silkworm more than four hundred centuries ago. Eventually their secret got out, and sericulture (silk production) travelled westward to Europe, with France leading the way. Through royal decrees and subsidies to encourage production, France dominated the industry from the fifteenth century until an epidemic wiped out silkworms in the mid-nineteenth century. Today, the majority of silk production is in China, Japan, and Brazil.

To produce high-quality silk you need two things: a moth (a Bombyx mori moth, to be precise) and a lot of mulberry leaves. The female moth lays between two hundred and five hundred pinpoint-sized eggs from which ravenous silkworms hatch and immediately start feasting. After a month-long binge on mulberry leaves, the silkworm increases in size 10,000 times! It then spins a very fine thread to make a cocoon, and begins its metamorphosis.

Inside the cocoon, the silkworm weaves a kilometre or so of filament, which will later be removed, unravelled, and spun into thread and knitted or woven into fabric. The best silk requires the finest and longest threads, but the moth damages the threads when it creates an escape hatch and makes its final journey to mothhood. That's why cocoons are steamed, boiled, or blasted with hot air before any such hatch can be made (which is very bad news for the silkworm).

Sericulture requires an unbelievable number of mulberry leaves, and making silk fabric requires a staggering number of cocoons. One acre of mulberry leaves feeds four or five silkworms, which means it takes approximately 225 cocoons, or fifty acres, to make a silk panty.

Today, the silk industry in France is hanging on by a thread, albeit a beautiful one, as it continues to design and manufacture crepe de Chine, muslin, georgette, chiffon, duchess, charmeuse, and satin.

Which came first, the fibre or the fabric? Fibre. No, fabric. (The answer is both, if the fabric's been recycled.)

Fibres are the smallest visible elements of fabric. Once collected, fibres are spun into thread or yarn and then used to make fabric.

There are mainly two types of textile fibres: natural and synthetic. Natural fibres grow in fields and on animals, and synthetic fibres grow in a chemistry lab. We generally assume that "natural" means good and "synthetic" is unnatural, or bad, and with words like eco-friendly, organic, recycled, and upcycled, it's easy to get confused.

How bad is "bad," and just how good is "good"?

A natural fibre, such as conventionally grown cotton, requires millions of litres of water and massive amounts of fertilizer and pesticides, and it leaves a gigantic carbon footprint on its field-to-mill-to-factory-to-consumer journey.

A synthetic fibre, such as polyester, is made from petroleum, a non-renewable, non-biodegradable resource that pollutes and causes global warming — all of which sounds terrible. On the other hand, polyester can be recycled. Think plastic bottles to fabric.

Fibres that are partly synthetic and partly natural combine both worlds and are referred to as semi-synthetic fibres, or regenerated fibres. For example, rayon is a regenerated fibre made using a chemical process that transforms cellulose found in wood pulp, a renewable resource.

Some fibres can also be made into same-name fabrics, such as cotton, because the fibres can be made directly into fabric, while other fibres need to be blended first, like spandex, which cannot be used alone. It's confusing at first, but once understood can help you decode the fabric content of any clothing label.

The list on the following pages gives an overview of the fibres most commonly used for lingerie, along with the upsides and downsides to the construction of fabric. Each fibre is evaluated according to its strength, wearability, absorbability, environmental impact, care instructions, and, perhaps most essential for any lingerie garment, elasticity. That doesn't mean how far the material can stretch, but the material's ability to recover its original shape *after* being stretched.

Natural fibres come from plants and animals.

COTTON: Cotton that's ready to pick looks like a popcorn plant! The soft, downy fibres grow on seeds inside a protected pod (called a boll) until there's no more room left and the pod opens, exposing fluffy fibres.

Advantages:

- Extremely comfortable, soft, and pleasant to the touch
- Strong and durable
- Best choice for very sensitive skin
- Absorbs moisture easily and breathes
- Biodegradable
- Easy care

Disadvantages:

- Creases easily and has to be ironed
- Little elasticity
- Colour dyes stay matte, so there are no shiny colours
- Conventional cotton produces a lot of pollution; look for organic cotton when possible

---

FLAX: Flax is the name of the plant used to make linen. The fibres are found at the base of the stem and are called bast fibres.

Advantages:

- Cool to the touch and very comfortable to wear
- Strong and durable
- Very absorbent, dries quickly, and breathes
- Good lustre, good drape, and doesn't cling
- Biodegradable
- Easy care

Disadvantages:

- Creases badly and needs ironing
- Little elasticity
- Processing can be environmentally unfriendly, depending on country regulations

SILK: This luxurious fibre comes from the cocoon of the silkworm caterpillar. The best silk comes from the domesticated Bombyx mori moth.

Advantages:
- 100% silk is the most luxurious material and feeling next to the skin
- High lustre and excellent drape
- Absorbent
- Some elasticity
- Rich, vibrant colours are possible because of high dye absorption
- Cool in the summer and warm in the winter
- Makes an excellent blend with cotton and wool
- Creases ease out while wearing

Disadvantages:
- Perspiration and sunlight weakens silk fabrics
- Silk is more delicate wet than dry, which is why gentle hand washing and dry cleaning are recommended
- The silkworm dies! "Peace silk" is not as common, but the fibre comes from cocoons where caterpillars have completed the transformation process to become moths, and have left through a hole in the cocoon

WOOL: This category includes wool from sheep and other animals, such as cashmere from goats and angora from rabbits.

Advantages:
- Naturally insulating — excellent fibre for blending with silk to create luxury thermal wear
- Excellent "wicking" properties, which draw moisture away from the skin
- Absorbent
- Breathes easily
- Excellent elasticity
- Biodegradable

Disadvantages:
- Shrinks easily
- Can be difficult to clean
- A coarse fibre that can be uncomfortable or itchy to wear
- Pills over time
- Dries slowly and is heavy when wet
- Stretches out of shape easily and has to be "blocked" back into shape after washing

Semi-synthetic or regenerated fibres are part natural and part chemical.

RAYON/VISCOSE: Rayon was the first manufactured fibre. It was developed in France in the late nineteenth century as a replacement for silk, which was too costly to produce in large quantities. Made from wood pulp and treated with chemicals, rayon is produced by the viscose process, by which a liquid solution is forced through a spinneret that looks like a showerhead to produce long filaments that are then hardened into fibres. The names *viscose* and *rayon* have become interchangeable.

Advantages:
- Soft and pleasant to the touch
- Inexpensive material
- Cool and comfortable to wear
- Moderate elasticity
- Highly absorbent
- Drapes well
- Luminous and shiny
- Biodegradable

Disadvantages:
- Creases easily
- Not very strong or long-lasting
- Highly flammable
- Requires careful laundering
- Dries slowly and can turn yellow with too much heat

MODAL: Modal is made from beech wood using chemical processing.

Advantages:
- Very soft and smooth with a natural and luxurious feel
- Highly absorbent
- Blends well with other fibres
- Good elasticity
- Doesn't crease easily
- Dyes well, so there are great colour options
- Easy care
- Biodegradable

Disadvantages:
- More expensive than viscose
- Creases easily
- Risk for allergic reaction from the chemical processing

LYOCELL: A form of rayon, lyocell is better known under the brand name of Tencel.

Advantages:

- Soft, lightweight, and very smooth, so it drapes beautifully
- Similar to viscose, but requires less chemical processing
- Strong and durable
- Moderate elasticity
- Highly absorbent

Disadvantages:

- More expensive than viscose or many eco-fabric alternatives
- Can pill over time

BAMBOO: Although bamboo is a natural fibre, it needs chemical processing before it can be spun into a suitable yarn to make fabric. Bamboo is the fastest-growing plant in the world and doesn't require any pesticides or fertilizers, making it a fascinating fibre to watch as it evolves in the future.

Advantages:

- Incredibly soft, smooth, and luxurious
- Absorbent and moisture-wicking
- Breathes easily
- Insulating — cool in the summer, warm in winter
- Anti-static
- Hypoallergenic
- Biodegradable

Disadvantages:

- Processing bamboo requires many chemicals, but it can be done in a closed-loop manufacturing circuit, which means that the chemical solutions are used over and over again
- Expensive

SYNTHETIC FIBRES

Synthetic fibres are 100% chemically engineered and mostly derived from petroleum. While this might sound like the apocalypse is near, it isn't.

POLYAMIDE (NYLON): An indispensable fibre for the lingerie industry. Most bras are made with a percentage of polyamide. Introduced in 1938 by Dupont under the trademarked name of Nylon, the name was later relinquished into the public domain to identify this new category of fibres and fabrics.

Advantages:

- Smooth, light, and very strong
- Good lustre
- Moderate elasticity
- Holds dye well
- Quick-drying, and wicks moisture away from the skin
- Resistant to perspiration
- Inexpensive

Disadvantages:

- Melts easily when ironed or dried on very high heat
- Stains easily
- Produces static
- Not biodegradable, but can be recycled
- Colours can fade in prolonged sunlight

ELASTANE/SPANDEX: Stronger and more durable than rubber, this synthetic fibre is known for its exceptional elasticity and can be stretched up to seven times its original length. Never used on its own, elastane/spandex is blended with other fibres.

Advantages:

- Strong fibre
- Improves crease resistance
- Gives fabrics greater comfort and ease
- Easy care

Disadvantages:

- Poor absorbency
- Avoid hot water temperatures during care (could weaken the fibre)
- Doesn't like chlorine: rinse bathing suits well after use

POLYESTER: Discovered in the 1940s, polyester is a completely synthetic fibre made from petroleum-based materials.

Advantages:
- Soft to the touch, so it drapes well
- Strong fibre that is durable
- Doesn't crease easily
- Very good elasticity
- Easy care — washes and dries effortlessly

Disadvantages:
- Doesn't absorb moisture very well
- Doesn't breathe well
- Not biodegradable, but can be recycled
- Difficult to iron — tends to melt or warp, but ironing is rarely necessary
- Can be itchy and scratchy

MICROFIBRES: The darling of the lingerie world, microfibres are ultra-thin (one-tenth as thick as a human hair) and give a luxurious look and feel to fabrics. They are mostly made from nylon or polyester.

Advantages:
- Very comfortable — your body feels cradled
- Strong and durable
- Good wicking capability, so it's a good choice for summer and active wear
- Resistant to staining
- Amazing elasticity
- Holds its shape and looks crisp and fresh throughout the day
- Easy to wash

Disadvantages:
- Not biodegradable
- Risk for allergic reaction from the chemical processing
- Can cause static

There are a lot of different fibres and fabrics, and the purpose of this list isn't to test or overwhelm you. The goal is to let you see and appreciate the decision-making that goes into fabric choices, which will in turn help you become more invested and feel more comfortable making your own clothing decisions. Practically, it also helps to become familiar with certain terms so that you can easily recognize them on fabric content labels.

$$\sim$$

A fabric label reveals the DNA of any garment. Forget the glossy paper and marketing vernacular. The good, the bad, and the ugly are all in the fine print, the really fine print, so grab a magnifying glass. Fortunately for lingerie, there are a limited number of components. Let's see what different labels might look like and what they mean.

LABEL A:
93% POLYAMIDE, 7% ELASTANE

WHAT IT MEANS: You'll see this combo a lot. Remember that polyamide is the generic name for nylon, and elastane is the same as spandex. If there is a lot of lace on the bra, this label also suggests that the lace is made out of nylon, which is a good thing. Lace can also be made out of polyester, which has a tendency to irritate the skin.

WILL IT LAST? Polyamide and elastane are the key ingredients for a basic, durable bra.

LABEL B:
LACE: 54% NYLON, 30% POLYESTER, 16% LYCRA / MESH: 84% NYLON, 16% LYCRA

WHAT IT MEANS: This label gives specific details for different parts of the bra, which indicates that it's well-constructed. Both the lace and mesh have high percentages of Lycra, which means strong elasticity. Remember, good lingerie moves with you, so the more elastane the better.

WILL IT LAST? The high-percentage of Lycra suggests a well-made, supportive bra.

LABEL C:
IMPORTED COTTON/SPANDEX

WHAT IT MEANS: This doesn't tell you much. The label indicates the bare minimum, which means there is likely nothing to boast about other than price.

WILL IT LAST? Probably not.

Based on what you now know about basic fibres and fabrics, get into the habit of reading fabric content and care labels. Having the right fabrics next to your skin will significantly enhance your lingerie experience. Textile regulations require fabric labels on all garments, making it easy to check if you are in the store. Online retailers, however, don't always provide this information in the garment description, so don't be shy about contacting them to find out. The more you know, the better decisions you can make.

The visual aspect of lingerie often overshadows the tactile experience. Reach out, touch, and feel the world around you. Starting tomorrow morning, consider the nutritional composition of both your breakfast and your lingerie, and then enjoy your day with every fibre of your being.

SEVEN

DETAILS & DELIGHTS

I consider lace to be one of the prettiest imitations ever made of the fantasy of nature; lace always evokes for me those incomparable designs, which the branches and leaves of trees embroider across the sky, and I do not think that any invention of the human spirit could have a more graceful or precise origin. — Coco Chanel

In France, I hear the word *sublime* pronounced *su-BLEEM* in French — daily. From the weather report announcing a spectacular day, to the description of a patisserie, to a neighbour recounting a vacation. The word is also often used to describe lingerie. Every season has a sublime colour and collection.

The meaning of *sublime* is the same in English as it is in French: divine, an overwhelming sense of awe inspired by great excellence, beauty, and emotion. However, it wasn't a word I encountered often before moving to France, other than in the expression "from the sublime to the ridiculous," which

I pronounced as one word, *fromthesublimetotheridiculous*. Eager to accomplish this and that, I was always more focused on *doing* than on *feeling*. I never experienced the space where sublime rests so I couldn't feel its full exaltation.

In lingerie, the sublime is in the details and their effects. Let's take a closer look at the artistry of the details that ultimately transform a bra — and our experience.

Lace and embroidery are two such details. To see their beauty you must look closely, carefully, and thoughtfully. Don't rush. It takes time to see and feel the sublime.

And determination and courage to make it.

A single night in December 1816 changed the course of lacemaking history forever. That's when three daring Englishmen dismantled and smuggled lacemaking machinery, called Leavers looms, across the rocky English Channel to Calais in France. They faced high risks, including capsizing, drowning — or getting caught, since exporting these new machines was a crime punishable by death.

Until Leavers looms came along, lacemaking was done by hand, a painstaking and intricate process of looping, braiding, and twisting threads to create an openwork fabric. The English were proud of their lacemaking machines, and eager to keep this industrial secret to themselves. The demand and the price were high for lace, the ultimate symbol of luxury.

Lacemakers are affectionately known as dream weavers, since lace is an illusion. What we see is the beauty and magic of our imagination. Both the background tulle and foreground motif are made simultaneously, creating subtle shading and intensity. Our eyes see a delicate pattern emerging and imagine that the threads follow the contours of these intricate designs, but in reality these threads can only move in two directions: warp (vertically) and weft (horizontally). A young mechanic, John Heathcoat, carefully observed the meticulous hand movements that created this effect and invented the first mechanical loom in 1804, which was improved upon by John Leavers in 1813. Finally, flawless and smooth mesh could be produced by machine.

Not everyone was pleased, especially the skilled cottage industry of lacemakers who feared for their jobs. They rioted, breaking into factories and destroying looms.

Sensing a business opportunity, the adventurous trio of Robert Webster, James Clark, and Richard Bonington set off with their industrial looms for France and a better future. Their timing was perfect. It was the end of the Napoleonic Wars, and the French aristocracy had returned with a need for luxury that fuelled a lace revival.

A few years later, Samuel Fergusson, another Englishman living in France, adapted the French Jacquard weaving loom, making it possible to create any pattern. *Et voilà*, an industry was born. By 1883 there were 10,000 employees and nearly 2,000 looms. In 1950, the small port town of Calais was the lace capital of the world, exporting 1,200 tonnes of lace annually. The industry has risen and fallen over the years, but it continues to weave dreams.

About those Leavers looms: they're big. Like, two and a half metres wide, twelve metres long, and twelve tonnes big. According to Olivier Noyon, President of Noyon Dentelle in

Calais, a fully loaded Leavers loom holds 60,000 kilometres of thread. That's enough to go around the world one and a half times. Oh, and it takes two months to thread. Try to remember that the next time you're struggling to thread a simple needle.

It takes a lot of grease to keep a loom like that in motion, and a highly skilled team working in synchronized precision. At the top of the ranks is the *tullist*, tulle-maker, who with the hands of a mechanic and the ear of a musician repairs everything from broken machine parts to broken threads.

Leavers looms have long ceased to be manufactured, so the lace today is made on machines that are over a hundred years old. It takes many years of apprenticeship for a tullist to really understand each machine, with its particular sounds and peculiarities. Leavers looms were never standardized, which means there's no twenty-four-hour customer service hotline or online chat forum to turn to when something breaks. Lacemakers rely on ingenuity, experience, and resourcefulness to solve problems. There is an enormous amount of pride for this métier, with families of lacemakers passing along the heritage, artistry, and *savoir faire* from generation to generation.

With 90 percent of the costs in the finished product coming from manual labour, good business sense would suggest surrendering to faster and cheaper methods for making more lace and more profit. However, lacemakers are artisans, and like artists, make art. Today, there are seven lace manufacturers, two hundred and twenty Leavers looms, and five hundred people employed in the industry in Calais.

Until Madame Annabelle asked me whether I wanted a bra *avec ou sans dentelle*, I had never really given the matter much thought, although I suppose somewhere inside me I leaned toward a dislike of lace, considering it fussy, dusty, and anti-quated. My grievances were ill-founded, though. Among them:

LACE SCRATCHES. Not Leavers lace! But poor-quality lace does. If you have sensitive skin beware of lace made with polyester. Leavers lace can be identified by the black-and-white registered trademark "Dentelle de Calais," and, more recently, the revived "Dentelle de Calais-Caudry" logo that features the emblem of a peacock with a fanned-lace tail. Always slide your hand beneath the lace to see how it looks and feels on your skin. If Leavers lace is outside your budget, polyamide (nylon) lace scratches less than polyester.

THE CHEAPER THE BETTER. Nobody sees it anyway! Do you really want to feel like a porcupine?

TOO MUCH MELODRAMA, CONTRADICTION, AND METAPHOR. From the provocative black see-through chemise for seduction to the white lace virginal wedding gown for walking down the aisle to black-veiled mourning attire, lace for me was a fashion detail indicating marital status: single, married, widowed. Now, it's anything but.

CAN'T TELL THE DIFFERENCE. True, at first glance, but like wine tasting, once you know what to look for you'll never drink a spritzer again. Good lace feels soft. The background netting has a tight weave and doesn't appear to be in the same dimension as the pattern. The lace pattern in the weave is clearly defined, like a high-resolution image rather than a blurry one. Good lace is woven. Look closely at the background netting: if it looks like a tic-tac-toe grid, the lace is better quality. Woven lace doesn't unravel when snared, which means you won't have to dash for your life like Cinderella.

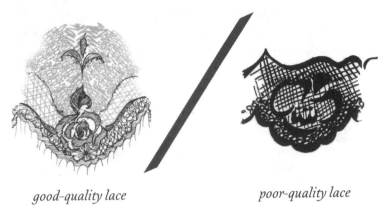

good-quality lace   *poor-quality lace*

Poor-quality lace feels rigid and likely has a nasty sheen. The background weave is wider and has larger holes. Often the lace pattern is spaced apart and the design looks chunky and blurry. Look closely at the background netting: if you see rounded loops, the lace is knitted and of lesser quality. Knitted lace unravels faster than light when snared.

If better-quality lace is just too expensive, but you still want the lace effect, avoid lace that contrasts with the colour of your lingerie. Stay within the same colour scheme — tone on tone — to add texture and detail in discreet harmony instead of attracting attention.

Expensive or not expensive, if you like it, great! Don't buy it just because you can afford it. If you don't like it, put it back.

TOO FRAGILE. Breaks easily. False! See above.

LACE IS SO YESTERDAY. *Au contraire*! Leavers looms have adapted with the times and textures, which has resulted in a number of remarkable innovations over the decades. Traditionally woven using cotton and linen exclusively, lace now includes nylon, Lycra, microfibre, and ecological fibres. Stretch lace is perhaps one of the most flattering innovations. Lingerie and lace designers work together to capture the emotions and sensations around us, creating unique designs that add intrigue and contour our bodies.

With similar effects, lace and embroidery are often used interchangeably; however, they are two very different processes. Lace is created as a fabric, woven as a whole piece, whereas embroidery involves using a needle to apply an ornamental motif on another piece of fabric.

The story of embroidery began in the small town of Saint Gall, Switzerland, where the textile tradition dates back to the twelfth century. A close network of farmers, spinners, and weavers worked together and successfully exported linen around the world. Fields covered with linen bleaching in the sun created a year-round winter wonderland with an illusion of snow-covered hills and earned Saint Gall the nickname of "the white city."

This enchanting image faded to black at the end of the eighteenth century when England started producing cotton, a cheaper alternative to linen. Saint Gall rallied, sourcing its own cotton and producing very fine and semi-transparent muslin. The introduction of hand embroidery soon led to an exquisite and delicate innovation — embroidered muslin — and launched a cottage industry of embroiderers.

The Industrial Revolution changed things, again. In 1828, Alsatian Josué Heilmann invented the first embroidery machine. Businessman Franz Elisäus Rittmeyer and mechanic Franz Anton Vogler, both residents of Saint Gall, later improved on this technology, and in 1883 another resident, Charles Wetter, discovered a chemical process that greatly improved and increased the production of guipure, often referred to as Venetian or guipure lace. Guipure is actually embroidery and is made using needles to stitch a motif on tulle, which in the past was painstakingly cut out by hand. The chemical process invented by Charles Wetter dissolved the tulle background. The combination of these nineteenth-century advancements assured the return of prosperity to the region.

The best embroiderers are still in Switzerland, where manufacturers have extensive archives for reference and inspiration. Embroidery continues to be a favourite embellishment for fashion and lingerie. The latest machines are technological wizards with each needle working independently to offer unlimited shapes, patterns, and colours. Embroidery can add strong graphical elements that are more pronounced than lace, and also creates relief for greater visual interest. One of the most enchanting design effects is embroidered lace, which combines the magic of both lacemaking and embroidery. The technique involves tracing the pattern in the lace with embroidery (often in a contrasting thread), creating an ethereal appearance and impression. Cutting-edge technology is pushing design, and designers are only beginning to experiment with the endless creative possibilities available with embroidery.

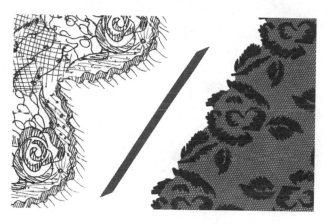

lace   *embroidery*

Before my Annabelle bra, I thought of details as unnecessary extras. I liked to keep things plain and simple. But I didn't see the lace on my Annabelle bra as unnecessary or extra. I saw it as an essential element to the bra. Completely integrated. Did the lace start where the fabric ended? Or was it the other way around? One depended on the other and the transition was fluid and natural, as was the nuanced path of light and shadow it created. And the delight.

What details do you notice on your bra? Next time you're out lingerie shopping, take some time to compare bras with a lot of lace or embroidery and bras without. Which do you prefer?

· III ·

UNDERNEATH IT ALL

THE ART OF WEARING FRENCH LINGERIE

❦

The art of pleasing oneself

EIGHT

DEFINING YOUR SILHOUETTE

Underpinnings for every shape.
— French proverb

Before profile pictures and selfies, there were silhouettes —
shadow portraits — made by shining a light on a subject,
tracing the shadow, and cutting the shape out in black paper.
I made a lot of silhouettes as a child, intrigued by how distinctive one's profile could be without any features.

In France, painted portraits were all the rage in the eighteenth century, but they were expensive. For those who
couldn't afford the real thing, a shadow silhouette was an
inexpensive alternative. The word is derived from Étienne de
Silhouette, a French finance minister whose unpopular efforts
to improve an austere economy earned him the reputation of
being a cheapskate. Too bad Étienne and his detractors aren't
around today to see how silhouettes have since been adorned

and become anything but cheap. I wondered if he'd be as confused as I was looking in the mirror and trying to identify my body type more than 250 years later?

❧

An apple? No, maybe a pear. I looked at the diagram and then back at me. Was I rounder on top or on the bottom? I couldn't tell. According to the pictures, I was either an apple, pear, triangle, inverted triangle, column, or hourglass. I sucked in my tummy and held my breath. Now I just looked ridiculous, and even a little purple. I let out my stomach and exhaled.

What was I doing referring to a bunch of mixed-up metaphors for a messed-up system of body classification?

Consider the first option: apple or pear. Who wants to look like the forbidden fruit responsible for the fall of Eden, or the ugliest fruit in a still life? As anyone who has ever made applesauce, apple pie, or cider can attest, there are a million different varieties of apples, so defining a woman's shape as "apple" is like applying the word "nude" to the same shade of makeup foundation for women of Nordic, Asian, African, or Hispanic origin. As for pears, they don't even get called on for fruit salad duty, probably because chances are high that the insides will be brown and mealy. Better to compare apples to apples, and leave the pears to pair with something else.

Perhaps your lineage is of a geometrical persuasion. If so, your body shape is a triangle or an inverted triangle. The influence of my father, a gifted mathematician, has me wondering if a triangle can be inverted? By definition, a triangle has three sides and three angles that add up to 180 degrees. In which case, how can there be an upside down or a downside up? And what kind of triangle? An equilateral, with three equal sides and three equal angles? An isosceles, with two equal sides and two equal angles? Or perhaps a scalene, with no equal sides and no equal angles? Different triangles = different body shapes.

Neither a fruit nor a triangle? Then maybe you're a column — which begs the question, what *kind* of column? Doric, Ionic, or Corinthian? Different columns = different body shapes.

If you're not a food group, trigonometric equation, or ancient architectural structure, you're an hourglass — an elite category for those with perfect body symmetry. Enviable, perhaps … but remember, an hourglass is also a timer, and time always runs out.

Let's recap: apple, pear, triangle, inverted triangle, column, and hourglass. There is nothing remotely elegant or inspiring about any of these body classifications. We desperately need a better language to describe our different shapes; our bodies deserve it.

Now let's take a look at how the French see themselves.

Instead of using fruit, geometry, architecture, and sand timers, the French prefer letters to denote shape: AVHXO. No mixed metaphors. No math. Five letters, which in and of themselves are beautiful shapes, but suggest even more. The real beauty of letters is in their power to create words, and with words comes language — a new language with less judgement and more emotion.

The five letters that follow describe the five different silhouettes and offer a new perspective and opportunity to discuss women's bodies and lingerie. I selected the words accompanying the letters to illustrate how important language is to inspire self-confidence. Feel free to keep the word if you think it applies, or find another one that works better for you.

$\mathcal{A}$ IS FOR ALLURE

DESCRIPTION: Defined by wider hips than shoulders, the A silhouette is reminiscent of the Eiffel Tower in all its elegance, majesty — and allure.

BRA SUGGESTIONS: Balance body proportions by drawing attention to the upper body. Wear bra styles with padding and straps attached to the side of the cups to increase the bustline. Balconnette, molded, half-cup, and bandeau styles can all be flattering choices. Look for horizontal patterns and lines, and sparkling materials to accentuate the shoulders and create overall harmony. Vary your tops and dresses to include wider necklines, such as the *bateau*, meaning "boat," which follows the collarbone from shoulder to shoulder; the Sabrina, named after the Audrey Hepburn movie, which is also a wide and shallow neckline but with slightly more curve; or the empire, which lengthens the waist and emphasizes the bust.

PANTY SUGGESTIONS: Wear high-cut styles, such as tangas, in ultra-light fabrics with spandex and in understated colours to slim hips and elongate legs. Detailing and embellishments in the front or back enhance natural curves without increasing volume. Soft, light colours capture grace and movement, and lace or mesh side panels can distract attention. Try wearing one size up for a smoother silhouette and overall slimming effect.

V IS FOR VA-VA-VOOM

DESCRIPTION: Defined by shoulders larger than the hips, V silhouettes have an elegant and statuesque shape with a generous bustline and a less pronounced derrière.

BRA SUGGESTIONS: Balance body proportions by drawing attention to the lower body. Molded bras create a smooth and natural bustline. Avoid horizontal stripes and styles that exaggerate what you already have naturally. Select straps with delicate details to soften the lines of this silhouette. Halter and plunging front and back necklines will dramatically highlight the symmetry of a V silhouette's shoulders, which will require bras with convertible straps to position accordingly.

PANTY SUGGESTIONS: Low-cut boxer styles and panties with scalloped edges will add detail and texture. Choose bold colours and patterns for balance and interest.

H IS FOR HARMONY

DESCRIPTION: Shoulders and hips are aligned, creating a balanced and elongated silhouette with a less-defined waist. Accentuating both the bust and hips will help create contours.

BRA SUGGESTIONS: Padded, push-up, frilly bras help shape the H silhouette. Cropped camisoles can add softness and gentle curves around the bust and hips.

PANTY SUGGESTIONS: French knickers with details on the side can create volume. Ruffled or ruched briefs visually add shape, while high-cut panties suggest a gentle roundness.

X IS FOR XTRAORDINARY

DESCRIPTION: Characterized by aligned shoulders and hips, the X silhouette has a well-defined waist with proportionate and balanced curves.

BRA SUGGESTIONS: Select well-constructed bras for support and gentle shaping. Choose daring V necklines and fabrics that follow

your curves. For greater definition, corsets, bustiers, pin-up, and retro styles look sensational on this silhouette.

PANTY SUGGESTIONS: Fashionable, retro-styled, high-waisted panties flatter and flatten if necessary, while a thong or scalloped-edged boyshorts and panties showcase your contours. Avoid ill-fitting clothing that is too loose, as it will tend to hide this symmetrical silhouette and make it appear shapeless.

O IS FOR OOH LA LA

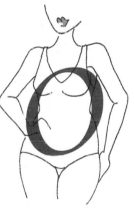

DESCRIPTION: An O silhouette has a volup-tuous bustline, with rounded shoulders and soft curves that include a tummy and hips. Draw attention to the upper part of the body with revealing necklines. Slender legs often accompany this body shape, so cre-ate intrigue with textured or coloured hosiery and leggings.

BRA SUGGESTIONS: Full-cup bras provide maximum shape and support, while half-cup and balconnette styles will sculpt a divine bustline. Be careful with minimizers that tend to flatten and spread out breasts instead of shaping them.

PANTY SUGGESTIONS: High-waisted panties in ultra-soft fabrics slim the hips while panties with a front panel provide support and help define the waist.

Remember, just because something fits doesn't mean it flatters — an important distinction when making any wardrobe choice. Size and shape are not to be confused or morphed into one another. Select styles that are unique to your body shape, and in a size that enhances the contours of your silhouette.

Stand in front of a full-length mirror wearing a bra and panty, and take a caring and discerning look at yourself. Which silhouette are you?

NINE

HIDE & PEEK

There is no light without shadow.
— Louis Aragon

French women are perfect, *oui*?

Actually, French women are body conscious too, just like the rest of us. However, their perspective allows them to enjoy what they have instead of dwelling on what they don't.

When I take American women on a lingerie tour of Paris, I start by asking them which part of their bodies they like best. This is a question that any child can answer without hesitation, but you take a group of grown women, some with advanced degrees, and all you get is silence.

Finally, a few grudging answers. "I guess I used to have good legs," says one.

"I'm in okay shape," says another, "for a mother of two."

"I've been told I have nice hands."

"My waist — ten pounds ago."

Nothing just *is* — without a qualifier, modifier, or justifier. When was the last time you gave yourself (or accepted) a compliment and didn't negate it with a "but"?

What happened to our younger selves, brimming with so much self-love that any reflective surface from a toaster to a windowpane was an opportunity to marvel at our magnificence? At some point as we age, we stop kissing our reflection and instead hop on the beauty-lies-within train, as if we must give up one for the other, never able to have both. Gradually, we learn to play down our nice attributes, as if embarrassed by them, and play up our faults instead. Or perhaps we have lost touch entirely with our assets.

For years I hid what I considered my oversized butt in roomy sweatpants, a bad habit picked up in high school to expedite the transition from class to sports. This routine continued well past student life and any need for a stop in the locker room. There were plenty of nice things about my body that I could have played up, but all I wanted to do was to hide that butt away.

Meanwhile, French women *mettre leurs atouts en valeur*, show off their assets. They don't slouch around in oversized sacks. A French woman knows how to *camoufler ses imperfections*, camouflage her imperfections, rather than overcorrect or tamper with *Dame Nature*.

One afternoon at the Louvre, I found myself staring at a painting of naked breasts, a flag, and a rifle — everything a girl needs to lead her country to democracy. It was Delacroix's 1830 painting *Liberty Leading the People*, and it captures all the romance and ecstasy of revolution.

The "Liberty" in this painting looks like a regular woman.

She could be any one of us. She is triumphantly holding the tricolour flag above her head with one hand and a rifle with another, seemingly unaware that her dress has slipped and her breasts are exposed and beautifully illuminated. (She's not wearing a bra, but how could she be? The bra wouldn't be invented for another sixty years.)

It's a stirring image. But if you pause to examine her — this real woman — you will also notice that she has thick ankles, a muscular and not very attractive neck, and there are corpses scattered at her feet. Nevertheless, she is breathtaking in her power and confidence.

How did Delacroix do that? I squinted. Lines blurred and details bled into puddles. When I opened my eyes wider again, I saw a composition of shapes and gradient light layering the intensity of textures and colours. I had never experienced the power of nuanced light and shadow before. If a little well-placed light on the breasts can draw attention away from corpses and thick ankles, surely I could find a way to lose the saggy gym pants.

Light and shadow can change your focus. Consider a cloudy, overcast sky. Compared to a clear blue one, you might think it's rather blah, making you feel likewise blah, or blah-er than usual. For some women, this is how they feel when they don't like what they see in the mirror. However, there is always profound beauty if you look more closely.

Let's reconsider that overcast sky. Even in a seemingly flat grey expanse there are patterns of light and dark. Squint, and the nuances become clearer. If you live in the country, look for a tree line. If you live in an urban setting, look at the city line. Rest your eyes on where the two meet (sky and trees, or sky and buildings). Notice how much more interest and contour there is now in the sky than when you saw it simply as a mass of one colour. Depending on the light and the time of day, the shapes between the trees or buildings are also defined. This is called negative space, and artists make great use of it in their compositions. Positive space is the subject of the image, and negative space is what surrounds it, but the two work in tandem.

There is nothing negative or positive about either negative or positive space; it's the singularity of focus that brings dynamic balance and harmony to the overall composition.

If light and shadow, and positive and negative space, have such a profound influence on how we view an image, perhaps this applies as well to how lingerie works in composition with the body.

It's a question of balance. Behind every perceived fault is an *atout*, an asset, waiting to be revealed or shown off, as the occasion dictates.

The French say *dessiner une silhouette*, draw your silhouette, and *gommer les imperfections*, erase the imperfections. No scalpel required! You only need a pencil and eraser to draw, smudge, blur, erase, and draw again.

LET'S PLAY!

The game of Hide and Peek masks a feature you're not too fond of in order to reveal the grace and allure of another one. The interplay of light and shadow will help you see yourself with gentle kindness so that you can delight in the beauty that has previously gone unnoticed.

HIDE: Large hips

PEEK: These curves likely outline a narrow waist

LINGERIE: Corsets. Not one from four hundred years ago, *mon dieu*! Try a waspie (waist cincher) or bustier to enhance a small waist with finesse. A bias-cut chemise in darker shades will also accentuate the waist and flow gently over the hips.

HIDE: Narrow hips

PEEK: Legs

LINGERIE: Full or half vintage slip with slit, either with lace or without. Lace will add another element of texture and shading to create intrigue.

HIDE: Generous breasts

PEEK: Sensual cleavage

LINGERIE: Bras with seams (those cut-and-sew bras I told you about earlier) for the best shaping and to smooth out any bulges. Look for a combination of lace and fabric to vary texture and light patterns.

HIDE: Small breasts
PEEK: A graceful neck and shoulders
LINGERIE: Triangle bras, bustiers, and camisoles reveal the curve and beauty of the shoulders. Strapless and halter-style bras work well for backless fashions. Look for delicate design details in bra straps that can often have the look of jewellery.

HIDE: Large derrière
PEEK: Small of the back
LINGERIE: Slips and chemises cut on the bias with a tapered back will flow beautifully, while light and shadow play in the undulating fabric. Panties with details and cutouts in the back are an appealing way to create shadow and light, and stretch lace will create interesting textured outlines.

HIDE: Flat derrière
PEEK: Legs
LINGERIE: Thongs will elongate and extend your leg. If you like stockings, try a garter belt or a ruffled panty with a built-in garter belt to draw attention to your legs.

HIDE: Too much tummy

PEEK: Arch of the back

LINGERIE: A chemise cut on the bias with a tapered back lace panel will offer a sensual night's sleep. During the day, look for a high-waisted, retro-style panty so the elastic doesn't cut into the part you're trying to hide. Panties with a centre supporting panel and sheer side panels and back will mask your tummy and create intrigue through textured shadows guiding attention to your low back.

Next time you find yourself starting to say, "I hate my . . . ," find the perfection that is hiding behind the imperfection; the positive in the negative space. Coax your radiance and beauty out of the shadows through contoured layering of textures, details, and cutouts. When you move, the shadows and light move with you in a delicate interplay, creating intrigue.

On my lingerie tours of Paris, I end by asking again, "What do you like most about your body?" This time, I hear a resounding chorus:

"My breasts."

"My legs."

"My neck and my shoulders!"

What do *you* love most about your body?

TEN

SIZE DOESN'T MATTER

We are all special cases.
— *Albert Camus*

Size mattered to me for a really long time. In everything. Large for ambition and dreams, and small for kittens and waists. Once I moved to France, size became an even bigger issue. Everything there was petite, except maybe the palace of Versailles. Jeans, espressos, beers, ice cream scoops, and macaroons were all *très* small. Even expressions had a regular and petite version. *Un peu, un petit peu*; a little, a small little — meaning a very small amount. *Un moment, un petit moment*; a moment, a small moment — the equivalent of "just a sec." *Le matin, le petit matin*; the morning, the little morning, for the wee hours.

Petite can also express intensity, as in *la petite mort*, meaning little death, an idiom for an orgasm so intense that you nearly die. And that, in France, is a *small* thing.

Sometimes petite can mean the opposite, as in "Madame has a *petit accent*," referring to how un-French my French sounded. When I wasn't causing auditory cacophony, I was bumping into everyone and everything, like a petite bull in a china shop.

I felt like an oversized outsider in so many ways.

But sizing doesn't exist in haute couture. That's because the best fashions are designed to the body. Remember that before the Industrial Revolution, clothes were custom-made and only the elite had access to the fabrics and seamstresses. Standardized sizing came about when it was necessary to scale production, so different sizes were attributed to certain measurements to accommodate as many people as possible.

Shopping habits changed and, over time, instead of tapering clothes to fit our bodies we began to taper our bodies to fit clothes. It's a numbers game, with women measuring their self-worth by a number on a label. And women are rarely content with their size.

We've all heard the statistic that 80 percent of women don't know their bra size. Who knows where and how this statistic originated, but it has been repeated so often that it has become a universal truth. It makes bra-sizing sound like nuclear science, and it makes women feel inept and unqualified to understand their own breasts. Part of the reason, as explained in chapter 5, is because different brands use different measurements and criteria in their manufacturing process. So let's forget about size and adopt an haute couture attitude instead. Knowing what to look and feel for in a bra will help you make better lingerie choices.

Start with the bra you are wearing right now. Yes, this is safe to try at home. Stand in front of a full-length mirror in your bra and panty. Wearing both of them together allows you to see and feel your body as a whole. While you're at it, smile. A smile makes everything seem better.

Now take your bra off. We're going to put it back on together.

BRA-VO: 7 STEPS TO WEARING A BRA THAT FITS

Here are seven quick and easy ways to guide you through choosing a bra that feels right.

1. CHECK THAT YOU'RE PUTTING YOUR BRA ON PROPERLY: Slip your arms through the straps, lean over, and let your breasts fall into the cups naturally. Don't forget that if the bra is new, you should fasten it on the loosest hook. The fabric will stretch over time, so you'll need to be able to tighten it. If you're wearing a bra you've had for a while, fasten it on the middle or tightest hook.

I can't put my bra on this way. If you're like me and latch it in front before sliding it back around and pulling the straps up over your shoulders, wiggle and jiggle a bit to make sure your breasts are completely inside the cups.

Stand up. Straight, like your mother told you, with your shoulders back. Slowing down the getting-dressed process even by a little bit helps bring focus to something that is often rushed. Most things work out better when given the right amount of attention. Maybe you are already looking at yourself differently, with more kindness.

2. CHECK THE CUPS: Are you spilling out over the top and sides of your bra? If so, the cups might be too small. Try a larger cup size. If you still encounter problems, perhaps the bra style isn't suited to you. For example, if you have fuller breasts and are wearing a balconnette or a demi, try a fuller cup that has more fabric and offers more coverage.

Are you floating around in cups that are puckering and wrinkling? Try a smaller band size. If the cup still wrinkles, try a smaller cup size. If you still aren't satisfied, try a different bra style, such as a half cup or balconnette.

You'll know that you're wearing the correct cup size when all of your breast tissue is completely inside the cups. Turn sideways and put your hand on your hip. Look for a slight shadow along the outside curve of your breast. Check to make sure that your underwire or the structure of your cup isn't pressing on this part. Turn and face the mirror. Check to make sure the gore, or centre front, is lying against your sternum, the part of your chest between your breasts.

Lastly, check your nipples. I'm sure they are in the right place anatomically, but is your bra holding them in the right place? Facing the mirror with your arms hanging loosely at your sides, check that your nipples are midway between shoulder and elbow.

3. CHECK THE BAND: Turn sideways in front of the mirror to see if the front and back of your bra is parallel to the floor. Your back band should be in the middle of your back. Ideally, if you were to trace the form of an equilateral triangle from the edges of your shoulders to the small of your back, your fingers would land on the band. If geometry isn't your strength, ask your partner, mother, daughter, sister, or friend to give you a hand. And while they're back there, ask them to check the tightness of the band by placing two fingers beneath it and pulling away from your back. If it's more than two centimetres, your band is too loose. The band should feel snug, but not suffocating. Offer to return the favour.

It's the band that does the heavy lifting, supporting and distributing the weight of your breasts.

4. CHECK THE STRAPS: Technically, the straps are the least important part of the bra. However, they still need to fit correctly. Check that your straps are lying flat against your shoulders. If they make an indentation, loosen your bra strap, and if they still leave a mark, try a larger band size. If your straps are falling off your shoulders completely, try tightening them, and if they continue to slip off, try a smaller band size. A good fit means that your straps feel good and they don't fall off. Try a racerback-style bra if your straps just won't stay up.

5. CHECK THE UNDERWIRE: If your bra has underwire, check that it lies flat against your rib cage and is aligned with your armpits.

6. CHECK YOUR DANCE MOVES: Raise your hands up over your head like you're at a rock concert. Go ahead, dance like you're front and centre! A bra that fits well will not budge while you shimmy and shake.

7. CHECK YOURSELF OUT: Take another look in the mirror. Head to toe. Turn a little to the right. A little to the left. No wonder you're smiling. *Magnifique!*

Follow these steps for every bra you own and you'll have a drawer filled with bras that measure up to your expectations. You'll feel great about yourself, or as the French say, *se sentir bien dans sa peau.*

ELEVEN

PANTY PERFECT

*Learn the rules like a pro,
so you can break them like an artist.*
— *Pablo Picasso*

On both sides of the Atlantic, there's a lot of panty pressure.

In America panties don't get much respect. "Don't get your panties in a twist," "I see London, I see France, I see (YOUR NAME's) underpants." Even the saying "Don't get caught with your pants down" suggests some dark, shameful secret lurking down there.

In Paris, panties get more respect, but that can lead to pressure of a different kind. You can be judged rather harshly for the kind of panty you wear. When I first moved, my new French friends gave me serious advice about what to put on for my first visit to the *gynéco* (pronounced *JEAN-ekko*, the short and friendly version for gynecologist). My *gynéco* was next to a Monop' (the short and friendly version for Monoprix, the ubiquitous half-department-half–grocery-store chain) in the heart of the fifteenth arrondissement on rue Vaugirard, the longest street in Paris. The first time I went there I clumsily knocked his extensive pencil collection off the corner of his Louis XVI desk, and my anxiety only worsened when I realized why my friends had been so insistent that I wear the right panties: there was a nice examining area with a real Persian rug, but no changing room. Not even a complimentary gown.

It's hard to believe that all this panty pressure is only a few decades old, like panties themselves. For centuries women went commando every day, not just on date night. *Panties just did not exist.* It was bad enough having to deal with all those hoops and petticoats when it came time to pee, without also having to move aside a panty when you squatted in the bushes (these were also the days before toilets and plumbing).

Catherine de' Medici tried to do something about the lack of panties, but she was way ahead of her time. The French queen loved to ride horses, and was desperate to get a little more coverage down there while mounting and dismounting, so she introduced *culottes*, closed-crotched pantaloons, way back in sixteenth century. Unfortunately, even the Renaissance wasn't ready for that level of panty etiquette, and women went back to wearing nothing.

Fast-forward to the eighteenth century. *Culottes* are now knee-length breeches worn by aristocratic men. In opposition, disgruntled working-class revolutionaries began to call themselves *sans-culottes*, without breeches, opting for full-length trousers instead.

Today's French expressions that use the word *culotte* are less derogatory than the panty lingo in English. The derivation of *culotte* from the word *cul* (meaning "ass," in all its proud vulgarity) is also related to the word *culot*, meaning base, and helps explain such expressions as *avoir du culot*, to have guts; *être culotté*, to be bold and daring; *porter la culotte*, to be in charge.

By the early nineteenth century, women wore long pantaloons, albeit *fendu à l'entrejambe*, split at the crotch, sparking delight amongst those fortunate enough to get a peek. Fortunately, as the century closed, so did the crotch. The iconic brand Petit Bateau is credited with creating underwear as we know; they began production in 1918 and continue to this day. Originally destined for children, the panty caught on with women, too, and over the next couple of decades manufacturers produced different-coloured briefs that varied in coverage.

It wasn't until the 1960s that bras and panties were made to be worn as a set. It still works this way in France — bras and panties stay together, both in the store and on the body, whereas, in North America, they are usually segregated: bras hang on mini-hangers in one section and panties are thrown into a bottomless bin elsewhere. But how can you possibly know how two pieces will look together *if you don't see them together*?

The most important word I learned once I moved to France was *dépareillé*. It means mismatched — as in wearing one kind of bra and another kind of panty. Before that, I had never considered the relationship (was there one?) between my bra and my panty. For French women, matching sets are an essential aesthetic. They bring a sense of harmony through co-ordinated design detail, and complete an artistic picture.

Understanding *dépareillé* and its subtleties explains the unique relationship French women have with their lingerie and their bodies. It's a rule, but that doesn't mean you can't break it — as long as you break it on purpose with intention and style. More than a wardrobe decision, *dépareillé* is an attitude, a philosophy — a way of life. You have the choice: to match, or not to match. It's like Hamlet's "to be or not to be" dilemma, except with bras and panties. As my neighbour once explained, "*Kate, il y a des choses honnêtes, mais pas légales.*" There are things that are honest, but not legal. You can choose to be *dépareillé* or not, as long as you know that you're doing it on purpose and not because you are behind on laundry.

For example, if you are a matchy-matchy kind of person, get in the habit of buying two panties with every bra. And if you buy two different panty styles, you'll get even more wear out of your bra by having that extra wardrobe option.

If you are *not* a matchy-matchy person, and you *like* the idea of being *dépareillée*, great! Just be sure to mismatch with style — your style. If anything goes, and that's the way you like it, you're all set. If it's complete anarchy above and below, here are some *dépareillée* suggestions to help you connect design elements and start mixing things up:

- LOOK FOR SIMILAR FABRICS. Select a common fabric such as cotton, jersey, or silk, and pair your bra and panty accordingly.

- LOOK FOR SIMILAR COLOURS. In French, *camaïeu* is a range of tones in the same colour family. This is a good way to go about mixing and matching.

- **IF YOU HAVE A SENSE OF COLOUR, USE IT TO CREATE CONTRASTS.** If you don't know the first thing about colour pairing, but love what you've selected, go ahead! Or if you would rather stay simple and chic, black and white will create a modern and contemporary look.

- **PAIR A SOLID BRA WITH A BOLD-PATTERNED PANTY TO GET OUT OF A FUNK.** A black bra with leopard-print panty, for instance.

- **MIX PATTERNS.** Polka dots and stripes, horizontal stripes and vertical stripes, flowers and abstract colours are all great places to start.

The point is to wear what you want, not just whatever's handy. You'll feel more connected to your body by giving thought to your lingerie selection, and there will be a ripple effect of that self-focus throughout the day.

The pages that follow contain descriptions and illustrations of the most common styles of panties. It is worth taking the time to try them all on (with the matching bras!) to see the whole effect and to feel the sensations offered by each.

BIKINI: Similar to a bathing suit bottom, a bikini panty sits well below the waist and has high-cut leg holes.

BOXER: An easy-to-wear style that covers both the hips and buttocks. With more coverage than the shorty, the boxer style is a popular choice for sports.

BOYSHORTS: Called the "shorty" in French, boyshorts just barely conceal the curve of the derrière. Covering the hips and sitting below the waist, this is a great style for low-waisted pants and other fashions.

CLASSIC PANTY: *Culotte* or *slip* in French, and panty or brief in English, this style provides full coverage front and back. Classic panties can be high-waisted or low-waisted, and are traditionally opaque in the back.

HIGH-CUT PANTY: In the past, a full-coverage panty was referred to as a granny panty. Brands have modernized the shape, creating retro looks with luxurious fabrics. The rise of shapewear has given the high-cut panty renewed popularity, as the form easily adapts to shaping and sculpting fabrics.

HIPSTER: In between a bikini and boyshorts, a hipster is a low-rise panty that hugs the hips and sits lower on the leg than a regular panty.

ITALIAN PANTY: A luxurious full-coverage panty, usually made with lace and embroidery in front, and a transparent mesh back to enhance texture and visual appeal.

TANGA: A tanga has a similar shape to a thong, but with a little more fabric everywhere, including the sides. Tangas have more surfaces for design details, such as cutout lace and sparkling materials.

THONG: Called a *string* in French, which is actually a more accurate description of these two tiny pieces of fabric connected by, oddly enough, a string. Also called a *cache-sex* in French, meaning genital cover, because despite not covering anything else, at least it does that. A mini-thong provides barely any coverage.

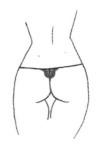

SEAMLESS: Any of the above styles that uses discreet materials and the latest technology, such as laser-cutting, to be invisible under clothing.

To have some fun with panties, I asked lingerie designer extraordinaire Paloma Casile to create a super-easy pattern. It's called the Paloma Panty, and if I can make it, so can you.

Trust me. Like all the suggestions and activities in this book, the fun and learning is in the doing, regardless of the results. I bet that once you've finished you're going to want to make more!

Paloma Panty Instructions

Materials

- Sewing machine
- Pins
- Scissors
- 50 cm stretch lace, tulle, or jersey (minimum width 90 cm)
- 20 x 20 cm cotton jersey for the crotch lining (you can also use a T-shirt!)
- 1 m of 7-mm width elastic with a decorative edge or ruffle
- 1 m of 7-mm width stretch lace trim
- Pattern. Scale the pattern according to the sizing guidelines.

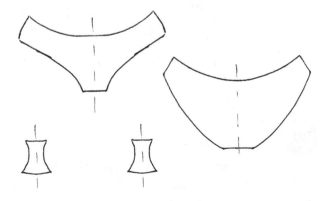

Step 1: Cutting the Fabric

Fold your fabric and pin your pattern pieces next to the fold. Make sure the stretch goes from side to side and not up and down. You will have one front, one back, and two crotch pieces. The second crotch piece will serve as a lining.

Step 2: Making the Panty

Place one of the crotch pieces right-side (the printed, pat-terned, or "pretty" side of the fabric) up on a table. Align with the back piece right-side up and the second crotch piece right-side down. Make sure the edges are lined up and pin.

Sew the three layers together using zigzag stitches.

Roll the back piece between the two crotch pieces and sand-wich the front piece right-side up between the two crotch pieces. Pin and stitch the three layers together.

Turn the crotch inside out. No visible seams!

Sew the side seams together.

Step 3: Sewing the Waistband Elastic

Measure the waistline of the cutout panty piece (or the pat-tern) and cut the length of the elastic 20 percent shorter.

Fold the elastic in half and mark the centre point with a pin. Mark the middle of both the front and back of the panty.

Place the elastic on the wrong side of the fabric and pin the middle of the elastic to the middle of the fabric. Use a zigzag stitch and sew as closely to the decorative edge as possible. As you are sewing, stretch the elastic slightly and hold down while you sew.

Continue until you have gone full circle.

Step 4: Sewing the Trim around the Legs

The steps for sewing the elastic around the legs are the same as for the waistband.

Cut the length of the trim 20 percent shorter than the leg opening.

Pin both ends of the trim to the inside of the leg and pin the middle of the trim halfway around the leg. Sew with a zigzag stitch.

Repeat for the other leg.

Step 5: Decorate!

Find a small bow or decorative detail and stitch in the middle of the waist.

Et voilà! That was easy, *n'est-ce pas*? Now you can make panties for every day of the week!

Paloma Panty Pattern

Enlarge pattern by 60%

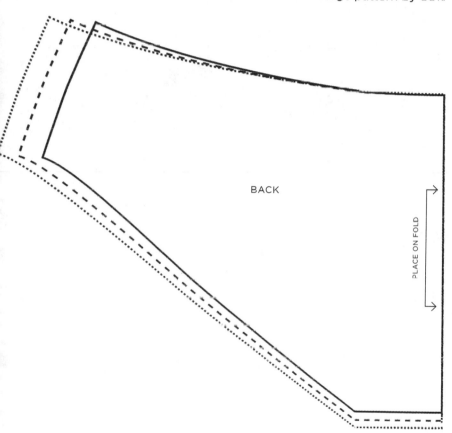

BACK

PLACE ON FOLD

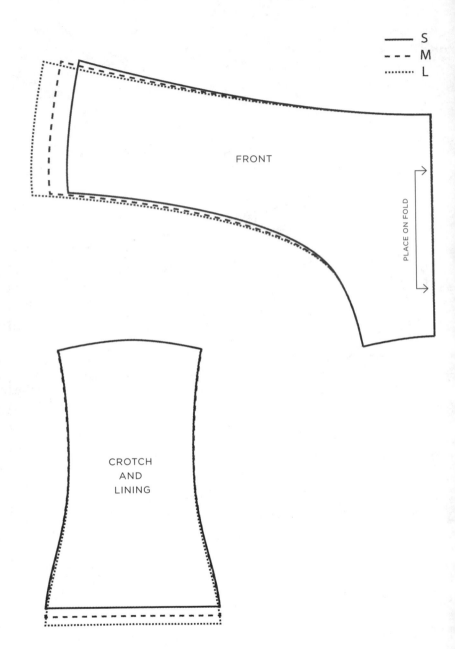

S

M

L

FRONT

PLACE ON FOLD

CROTCH
AND
LINING

TWELVE

GARTER BELTS & STOCKINGS

Some things are hidden so as to reveal them more.
— *Michel de Montaigne*

It could have been the Canadian winters, or the Lycra crew shorts and racer-back tank top to which I was partial in summer. Whatever the reason, or the season, I seem to have missed the conversation about the importance of garter belts and stockings.

The purpose of those intimate items remained abstract to me, and nonessential to the meaning of life. I was more concerned with my career options and marrying my college sweetheart (who hadn't voiced an objection to growing old with me in pantyhose).

Then my husband and I moved to France, and everything changed.

We were out at the famed Moulin Rouge with our new French friends, Pierre and Armelle. I watched as the dancers can-canned their way across the stage, all synchronized hips, their legs in hitched-up stockings.

"To the *belle époque*!" enthused Pierre as he refilled our champagne glasses.

"Amazing," said my husband, glassy-eyed after the number ended.

I looked from one to the other. "I love the costumes," I admitted, "but I don't envy the dancers having to lace up those corsets or struggle with those stockings every night. What a hassle!"

It was then that Armelle dropped the garter guillotine. "*Chèrie*," she said, leaning toward me, "any woman who truly loves her man wears stockings."

Gulp.

After that, I began to notice garter belts and stockings everywhere: soirees, cafés, at the gym, on the street. And, of course, in window displays of the ubiquitous lingerie boutiques throughout Paris. There were a lot of women in love, including *moi* — and I was going to prove it *à la française*. I began to take an active interest in what I had formerly dismissed as "hassle-wear."

A little research revealed that the French word for garter belt, *le porte-jarretelles*, stemmed from two words: *la jarretière*, a ribbon or band that was used by both men and women to hold up their socks behind the knee (*le jarret*); and *le porte*, a holder. The clips attached to the bottom of the *jarretelles*, garter straps, hold up the stockings.

While my friends were defending their Ph.D.'s, attending leadership seminars, and learning Photoshop, I signed up for, yes, a garter belt workshop. Cervin, the legendary French hosiery manufacturer, organized an *Atelier Porte-Jarretelles*. I showed up on a Saturday afternoon at their showroom basement, which had been converted into a speakeasy for the occasion. That's where I met Julia Palombe — a singer, model, and dancer — who greeted us (un)dressed in a black bustier, retro panty, black garter belt, and blush stockings.

The first order of business was a flute of champagne because, well, this was Paris. Then we moved on to introductions. There were three other participants, all women, none of whom looked as if they needed *Garter Belts & Stockings for Dummies*. Two of them, twins in their mid-twenties, were dressed à la pin-up in identical pencil skirts and stockings. Their only apparent difference was their chosen shade of lipstick: one had on a deep blue-red, the other was in a brighter, tomato-y red. They loved everything retro and the idea of an afternoon at a speakeasy sounded fun.

A photographer was also on hand to capture our magical moments. She was wearing an aqua flounce skirt, the straps of her garter belt visible beneath and attached to a pair of black opaque stockings with grunge-gaping holes.

Meanwhile, I was in jeans and socks.

"A garter belt is more important to me than a bra," said Julia. "It's not a fashion accessory. It's a lifestyle. A beautiful bra makes me feel great, but a garter belt and stockings make me feel sensational." To me, sensational meant a day on the ski slopes followed by a deep-tissue massage. "This is the front and this is the back," she continued, turning the garter belt over, sending the straps flying through the air and clinking like chimes. "Ideally, there should be six straps."

"Six sounds excessive," I said, looking up from my note-taking. "Why not four?"

"Six holds everything in place so that your stockings do

not fall down," said Julia. "Don't worry, they move with your body. You will feel a gentle tug from time to time, just enough to remind you."

"Remind me of what?"

Julia's eyes twinkled. "That life is full of unexpected pleasure."

While the pin-up twins mugged and posed for the photographer, I had Julia all to myself. "Why don't you try?" she said, handing me the garter belt.

"Um, okay."

I stepped behind the screen and shimmied out of my jeans. I put the garter belt on back to front, as I do with my bras, and twisted it around.

"Now the stocking," said Julia. "Sit down on the chair and slip it over your foot. You must secure your foot, or your stocking will not be straight and the seam will zigzag up the back."

I adjusted my toes and heel so they were aligned in the reinforced foot of the stocking. I had grabbed the top to pull it up when Julia cried out, "*Mon dieu!*" as if stricken. She put her hand firmly on mine. "It is not a sock," she cautioned. "Unroll the stocking slowly and coax it up your leg. Use the pads of your fingers, or your nails will catch. Feel the seam in the back to guide you."

I tried to do what she said. I coaxed, I pleaded, I cursed. Feeling ridiculously campy, I realized that I had more chance of winning the Nobel Prize than having a career as a B-movie seductress. By the time I got the stocking up and the seam centred, beads of perspiration had dripped down onto my forehead.

"Now what?" I said, clinging to the top of the stocking.

"Now you are going to attach the clips, like this," said Julia, taking hold of one of hers to demonstrate. "To open the clip, hold it like so, between your index finger and thumb. Use your index finger to slide the clip up and out. See?"

Yes, I could see. There was nothing wrong with my sight. My dexterity was another matter. I was practically using my teeth on the clips by the time I had wrangled one open.

"It takes a little practice," Julia reassured me. "Attach the back strap first. It's easier. Let the straps sit slightly to the side instead of straight back. Think of a clock. You want the back strap to be at five o'clock on the right thigh and seven o'clock on the left so the clips don't poke you when you sit down."

I reached behind me for five o'clock but must have been closer to English Tea Time, because Julia gently moved my hand further back.

"Clip on the welt, the darker band, about an inch from the top," she said.

Surprising myself, I eventually attached all six clips. "*Très bien*," confirmed Julia. "Now adjust the straps to your leg length. Give yourself a bit of slack in order to sit down. It helps to lift your leg onto a chair to adjust."

I hoisted my leg like Marlene Dietrich, gaining confidence all the while, and then repeated the entire procedure on the other leg.

"*Et voilà!*" I said proudly.

Julia took in the full picture, frowning at the wingtip oxfords I had kicked aside. "You need heels," she admonished. "Try mine."

Standing tall in Julia's red patent leather pumps, my back slightly arched, I teetered before I found my balance. I looked with surprise and pride at my reflection in the mirror.

Except that I had to pee. Badly. All that champagne.

Julia handed me a silk wrap and directed me toward the rest room. I rushed into the cubicle and realized that I had a problem. I couldn't pull down my underwear, which was stuck at stocking level and trapped beneath the garter belt, straps, and clips. I had no idea how to disentangle myself, and I was running out of time. I crossed my legs and jiggled to avoid disaster and hurried to unfasten all six clips. Three broken fingernails later and accident averted, my stockings now lay bunched around my ankles. I yanked them (no coaxing this time) back up my leg, attached them as best I could, and bounded back to Julia.

She took one look at the misaligned wreckage of my stockings and clasped my hands. "Wear your panties on top if you're going to wear a garter belt all day," she said with a smile. "It will be a lot easier, *n'est-ce pas*?"

"But all the photos and window displays show the underwear underneath!"

"A preferred marketing aesthetic," said Julia. "Wearing a garter belt and stockings all day is different. And in the game of seduction, they're more appealing than panties and should be the last things to go. There is another option, of course."

"What's that?"

"No panties at all."

Oh dear God. There was still so much to learn.

WHAT IS A GARTER BELT? A garter belt is an essential item in every woman's lingerie drawer — along with stockings, *bien sûr*! Made of silk, satin, lace, and fabrics that preferably have some stretch, a garter belt fits around the waist and sits on the hips. Attached to the belt are straps with clips at the bottom for fastening the stockings. Many women unjustly blame their stockings for falling down or sagging; more often, this is the result of wearing an ill-fitting garter belt.

HOW TO CHOOSE A GARTER BELT. Look for a garter belt that fits snugly on the hips. Too loose, it will twist around. Too tight, it will compress. If you have to attach it on the loosest setting then the belt is too small.

Ideally, there should be six straps for better support and to prevent the stockings from sliding down. Metal clips are better than plastic, which break easily, or silicone, which tend to bunch up the stocking and twist around.

If you're looking for a little more support, try a garter belt with a control panel or waist cincher that flattens and shapes your waistline as well as holds up the stockings.

WHAT ARE STOCKINGS? Stockings are made of 100% silk, 100% nylon, or either in combination with Lycra. They cover from the toes to the thighs. If you have never experienced them, they are quite unlike pantyhose, where the crotch sits cradled between your knees or the waist is so high you could pull it over your face and rob a bank.

There are several types of stockings, including:

Fully-fashioned: Knitted on flatbed machines and sewn together at the back, fully-fashioned stockings leave the signature seam that has come to symbolize authenticity and elegance. Look for the "keyhole" on the back of the welt (the darker top part of the stocking). The keyhole shape forms during the manufacturing process and occurs when the top of the stocking is folded back onto itself and stitched down.

Regular: Either 100% nylon, or with a touch of Lycra, and knitted on circular cones instead of on flatbed machines, regular stockings have no seam.

Mock-seamed: The same as regular stockings, but with a seam added on afterward as a design detail to resemble a fully-fashioned stocking.

Hold-ups or stay-ups: A popular choice because of their simplicity. Silicone bands hold the stocking in place, so there is no need for a garter belt — in theory. Depending on the shape of your thigh, stay-ups can either grip too tightly, or not enough. In the case of the latter, you are liable to be at a dinner party when you feel the discouraging sensation of your stockings rolling suddenly down your legs only to coil at your ankles. If you do find a brand that works for you, buy several pairs! Stay-ups are a great alternative to pantyhose.

WHAT DOES DENIER MEAN? The transparency of a stocking is measured in deniers. A denier is the measurement of fibre thickness based on a standard mass of 1 gram per 9,000 metres. The lighter the thread, the lower the denier, resulting in greater transparency. Conversely, the higher the denier, the thicker the thread and the greater the opacity. Transparent stockings range from 15 to 20 deniers, which give a beautiful sheer finish and a slimming effect. Opaque stockings can range from 40 to 180 deniers.

HOW TO CHOOSE STOCKINGS: For spring and summer, you'll need 7 deniers for the sheerest of the sheer, and 10 or 15 deniers for a soft and ultra-light feel. Toss them in the air and they'll float back down. For fall and winter, you'll likely want a stocking between 20 and 40 deniers, and if you prefer opaque, look for a stocking between 40 and 180 deniers. Remember that packaged stockings are folded over and over again, which changes and intensifies the density of the colour and doesn't reflect the opacity on your leg. Test the colour using the samples in the store and slip your hand in to see the effect on your skin.

IS SILK REALLY BETTER THAN NYLON? The answer in general is yes...but not necessarily when it comes to stockings. Silk is a natural protein fibre that helps keep you warm in the winter and cool in the summer. The luminosity of a silk stocking also adds to the luxury. However, silk stockings feel abrasive compared to nylon and make a rustling noise when your legs brush together. These can either be reasons to love the vintage feel and aesthetic of silk stockings, or not.

The most popular choice is 100% nylon — without any stretch. That's right. No Lycra! Pure nylon creates a contour that defines the leg, bringing attention to the centre and creating a slimming effect with transparency and light. Stockings with Lycra tend to flatten the leg, making it look larger, shorter, and wider. "*Ça boudine!*" as Julia would say, like sausages.

WHAT DOES RHT MEAN? Reinforced heel and toe. The advantage is that the stocking won't twist around. There are different styles of reinforced heels: French Point, Cuban, Manhattan, and Havana. Under no circumstance should you wear these with open-toed shoes!

French Point: An elongated and delicate shape that comes to a point — *très chic*.

Cuban: A vertical, rectangular shape that adds a graphic element contrasting in colour to the rest of the stocking.

Havana: A shorter, wider version of the Cuban heel, the Havana style is less common than the others, and was popular in the 1940s and 1950s, making it all the rage among vintage-wear aficionados.

Manhattan: A fancier design that has a decorative outline around a form that is similar to the Cuban, but finishes in a point instead of a squared-off top.

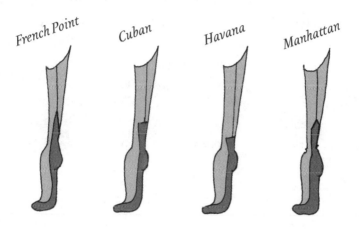

French Point Cuban Havana Manhattan

HOW DO I KNOW MY SIZE? Sizing in stockings takes into consideration your shoe size and height. A fully-fashioned stocking (without any stretch) needs to be the real length of your leg. That means it will look exceptionally long when you pull it out of the package. The volume of your leg will fill in the stocking and, ideally, the underwelt (just below and slightly lighter than the welt but still darker than the stocking) will be mid-thigh, with the welt slightly higher.

HOW TO PUT ON STOCKINGS. Take the stocking in your hands with your thumbs on the inside and gather it up between your fingers. Slip the stocking over your foot, taking the time to place the seam and toe correctly. Once your toes and heel are anchored, gently pull up the stocking, guiding the seam along the way so it stays centred. Starting with the back strap, attach the stocking about an inch from the top of the welt. Remember to keep the strap slightly off to the side of your thigh instead of straight back. Attach the front strap next and then the side, if your garter belt has six straps. Next, adjust your straps, remembering to allow a little give in order to sit down comfortably. Finally, cup your foot with both hands and then pull them up your leg to mold the stocking to the shape of your leg. Slight folds at the ankles indicate authentic stockings, but you shouldn't wind up with elephant ankles. If you do, the stockings are too big. Check to make sure your foot size is correct.

Stockings should feel taut. If they aren't, either the stocking is too big, or the garter belt straps are too long and need to be adjusted.

Note: nylon stockings can resist almost any tug-of-war, but be careful not to snag it with a fingernail! Wear gloves to avoid tearing, or apply a moisturizing cream first to soften your skin. (An advantage to nylon stockings is that if they do snag, the hole won't spread any further — unlike with a stocking made from Lycra.)

WHAT SHOES TO WEAR? In general, your legs and stockings look best with high heels. Traditionally, a French Point looks best in *talons aiguilles*, a fine-heeled shoe, while a Cuban heel looks best in a shoe with a more graphic, architectural heel. If you are wearing stockings with a coloured seam and RHT, do not hesitate to wear a shoe of the same colour. It helps continue the line of the seam.

WHAT CLOTHING TO WEAR? Your style is yours to define, so try different ways of wearing stockings until you feel comfortable. If you like shorter skirts, make sure the welt doesn't show. Remember, the idea is to create an allure and stir the imagination, not give too much away. And, of course, try wearing stockings under your jeans for a glammed-up casual. The lump of a garter belt clip underneath tighter clothing is often less marked than you think, and undeserving of its fashion faux pas status. *Au contraire*!

Whatever your choice, whatever your style, enjoy the freedom and pleasure that wearing stockings brings.

THIRTEEN

FAUX PAS

I have nothing to hear from an ungrateful
and false friend. — George Sand

We all have bra troubles and make bra mistakes. There's a mine-field of obstacles out there if you believe everything you read. The plethora of products on the market that offer salvation reads like a list of surgical supplies: breast pads, body tape, nipple covers. I know because I used to sell them.

I, however, thought I was selling bra solutions. Along with fabric wash, Soyelle offered an extensive range of lingerie accessories designed to provide the right fix for any bra and every related problem. I recognized, of course, that I wasn't solving world hunger, but I did believe that I was helping thousands of women in small, sometimes invisible ways. And once I started looking, there was no end to the help I could provide; there were problems everywhere. Everything became an issue: small breasts, large breasts, uneven breasts, sagging breasts, falling bra straps, visible bra straps, digging bra straps.

One such perplexing challenge was to find a way for women to quickly hand wash their lingerie while travelling. I came up with unidose — a single dose of fabric wash covered in a soluble wrapping that dissolved once in contact with water. It was the perfect product. With visions of unidoses dancing in my head, I headed off to pitch my new invention at Printemps, one of France's major department store chains.

Sitting across from the buyer in a small, dimly lit supplier-meet-buyer cubicle at the head office in the outskirts of Paris, I launched into a series of possible lingerie misfortunes.

"Imagine if the airline lost your suitcase? Or if your flight was late and your period was early?" I said, before elaborating on the immeasurable damage caused by salt, chlorine, and sunscreen, all ravaging bathing suits by the minute. "The unidose is ideal for women on the move — dynamic women, like your clients," I concluded, convinced that I'd nailed it.

"Perhaps," the buyer said. "But you've forgotten that we are in the dream business."

I had, indeed. Instead of alleviating problems for women, I was compounding them.

In the months that followed, I reviewed our catalogue and communications materials. Every product had its place as long as it didn't stop women from dreaming just a little.

Then, as a consumer, I started to practise what I preached. Let's take a closer look at some of these so-called problems and their so-called solutions.

ADHESIVE BRAS Sticky buns, okay, but a sticky bra? Make sure your reason for wearing a stick-on bra truly merits the missed opportunity of wearing a real bra and feeling the caress of soft fabric next to your skin. Ask yourself how embarrassed you would be if it fell off on the dance floor.

BORING SHAPEWEAR Of course you want to feel good in what you're wearing, but that doesn't mean you have to accept uninspiring shapewear. Design has greatly improved, so look around for some different options with colour, lace, and texture effects. Remember, shapewear is still part of your lingerie wardrobe, not your yoga wardrobe.

BRA EXTENDERS These little pieces of extra bra strap hook on to your bra closure to lengthen the band. While bra extenders might give you some more breathing room, make sure that you're breathing for the right reasons. Some commercial arguments may suggest that bra extenders are a great solution for "half-sizes." Maybe, but if you need more room, try a larger band size (remembering to go down a cup size — refer to the sister sizes chart in chapter 5). Bra extenders can be of help during short periods of weight change, such as in pregnancy, so that you can wear your favourite bras longer.

BRA PADS Who has never padded the truth before? Bra pads are great for adding a little lift and shape here and there, but remember what happened to Pinocchio's nose when he lied excessively. You don't want your cleavage to look like a bad cartoon.

INVISIBLE STRAPS There is nothing invisible about invisible straps! They look and feel like the underbelly of a dead fish. The allure of a beautiful bra strap is in its elegant simplicity or intriguing detail, which is always better than silicone — or worse — yellowed silicone. And if your strapless bra won't stay up without straps, it's not doing its job.

LINGERIE ETIQUETTE Enough with the cutesy talk: stop referring to your breasts as "the girls." Think of the expression, "If it looks like a duck, walks like a duck, and quacks like a duck, then it's a duck." Breasts are breasts. It's a great word.

MINIMIZERS Breasts too big? Sure, you can minimize with a minimizer bra that "reduces" your bra size by flattening your breasts like pancakes, but the visual effect is a squared-off version of your torso that adds unnecessary dimension and leaves little distinction between your breasts, waist, and hips. It's better to wear a well-constructed bra with seams and side panels to shape your breasts and bring them forward, creating a more flattering silhouette with a more defined waist.

NIPPLE COVERS Women might wear nipple covers for several reasons. Some, who have extremely sensitive nipples and can't stand the feeling of fabric rubbing against them, use small, petal-shaped or round covers. Others wear nipple covers because they feel self-conscious about nipple visibility under clothing and would prefer more discreetness. Like the adhesive bra, ask yourself why you need them. Make sure it's your choice to cover up, not because of any suggestion that you should.

NUDE BRA Dull. Do you want every day of your week to be beige and invisible? Lingerie is capable of turning ordinary into extraordinary, if you let it.

SHOULDER PADS I'm not talking about the padded variety from the eighties, the kind that broadened and squared off your shoulder to resemble the stature of a man. Today's shoulder pads are often made of silicone to prevent slipping, and are referred to as "cushions." Their mission is to protect your skin from chafing beneath your bra strap. If your straps are digging in to the point of pain, they're doing more heavy lifting than they should be. The real culprit here is likely your back band, which is too big. Try going down a band size (and, all together now: up a cup size!) to see if you are relieved of some of the pressure on your shoulders and feel a more balanced weight distribution around your torso.

TAPE Tape is an office supply, not a lingerie accessory. Often called fashion tape, it's worn by posing and camera-ready celebrities with plunging everything. If the risk of a falling piece of fabric is so critical that it needs to be super-glued, then it's likely you'll spend more of your evening worrying about coming undone than ensconced in conversation or dancing insanely.

T-SHIRT BRAS Yawn. The name alone is so uninspiring, and we have only ourselves to blame. Playing into the practical psyche and desire for a smooth look underneath tighter clothing, the term *T-shirt bra* was coined to make women feel more comfortable in their bra purchase and vocabulary. *T-shirt bra* is non-sexual, non-judgemental: it's safe — except safe is void of any notion of sensuality, focusing on being solution-based instead of sensation-inspired.

There is a fragile balance between what is practical, imaginary, and real. Lingerie helps preserve this balance and instill pleasant sensations in what is otherwise quotidian. No matter how perfect the solution, if what you're wearing doesn't delight, don't wear it.

A BOUDOIR OF ONE'S OWN

CREATING YOUR
LINGERIE WARDROBE

❧

A whisper of lace, a shadow of mystery,
and the caress of silk

FOURTEEN

YOUR LINGERIE & *TOI*

Change your life today. Don't gamble
on the future, act now, without delay.
— Simone de Beauvoir

Each spring, I look forward to a particular invitation — not to the Élysée, the home of the president — but somewhere better. I get invited to judge the final student collections at ESMOD Paris, the oldest fashion school in the world, founded in 1841 by the tailor Alexis Lavigne, who invented the mannequin and soft measuring tape.

I always look forward to seeing the work of young, creative minds not yet tarnished by the realities of real-world bosses and budgets. To graduate, students present their lingerie collection before a jury. (They also double as models for each other's collections.)

My role as juror is to evaluate the collections on their creativity, technical merit, and business and marketing plans.

Each student gets ten minutes to present. They begin with a *planche d'ambience*, an inspiration board, which is a collage of images, colours, and fabric swatches that tell the story of their vision.

There's a strong correlation between inspiration boards and the most promising designers. It's not just about the best illustrations, dazzling Photoshop effects, perfect stitching, or immaculate seams. As with good books, it's not always the prettiest writing that holds our attention but the best story. The most impressive lingerie collections invoke a compelling narrative, and that narrative begins with a mood, a feeling, an emotion.

Emotion. The word was first used to describe a public disturbance in the sixteenth century. Five hundred years later it has morphed into blinking, winking digital emoticons that overwhelm our computer screens and cellphones. Derived from the French *émouvoir*, which means to agitate, stir up, and excite, *emotion* has only within the last two hundred years been linked to feelings or used to describe physiological expressions. The distinction between emotions and feelings continues to stir debate among neuroscientists, scholars, psychiatrists, and anyone trying to understand their relationship with their mother.

The relationship between emotions, feelings, and lingerie is what matters to us. Lingerie doesn't just cover the body, lifting here and pushing there. It caresses us and ignites strong reactions. Annabelle knew it, Gentry de Paris knew it, and these fashion students knew it, too.

I remember one student's collection in particular — inspired by the poetic undertones of Stendhal's view of nascent love and its outward expression in *De l'amour* (*On Love*). Stendhal had been intrigued by the crystallizations at a salt mine near Salzburg, Austria, particularly by the beauty of a single branch after the salt water had dried and left it cloaked in shiny deposits. For Stendhal, this illusion of diamonds was the perfect metaphor for the stages of love. The student's interpretation of Stendhal's words — "I call 'crystallization' that action of the mind that discovers fresh perfections in its beloved at every turn of events" — resulted in a breathtaking collection, composed of diaphanous layering and silver and winter-white tone-on-tone patchwork of leather, lace, and silk, with shimmering crystal accents to illustrate the transformation of the ordinary into glittering perfection as one falls deeply in love.

Over the years of listening to students and observing their collections, I have learned that we are all designers of our own femininity and sensuality, which ultimately finds expression in our lingerie. But when it comes to getting dressed every day, many women give little time or thought to their lingerie selection. They go through the motions without the emotion.

Let's break that routine.

FIFTEEN

CREATING A LINGERIE JOURNAL

Creativity takes courage.
— Henri Matisse

In this section we are going to work extensively on your lingerie journal. Every designer I know carries one to capture fleeting ideas and inspiration. Fortunately, you don't need to be a designer to keep a lingerie journal; I certainly wasn't when I started mine. Part notebook, part diary, part art journal, part stylebook, my own lingerie journal has evolved over the years — and continues to do so. It is a creative place and space in which to observe and explore the layers of the complex world of sensations, textures, feelings, emotions, and reflections. You can enjoy lingerie so much more when you bring real awareness to it instead of simply going through the motions.

This is more than a journal about pretty small things. Think of your lingerie journal as *les dessous de la créativité*, the foundation of creativity (with a play on the word *les dessous*, which also refers to foundation garments and underpinnings). Creativity is an invitation to play and a chance to be more tolerant and free of expectations. Instead of focusing on things we "should" do, we begin to explore the endless possibilities that open up when we think of things we "could" do. There is no right way or wrong way to work in your journal — only curiosity and a desire to have fun on every page.

These pages offer an opportunity to reflect on what lingerie means to you; how to identify areas for change; and how to integrate a new approach, attitude, and habits. You are free to write what you want, how you want, and when you want. My only advice is to find a quiet place both physically and mentally. As you fill in the pages, you'll inspire joy, find pleasure, gain insight, increase your self-awareness, and develop a new perspective on your lingerie.

Take. Your. Time.

By the end of the process, you will have put into words how you want to *be* and how you want to *feel* in your lingerie. And on the practical side, you will have interpreted your desires and needs for every occasion, whether curled up with a good book or expecting company.

Use these pages as prompts to prep your own journal. Do whatever works best for you — after all, this is your journal. Each page is part of a treasure hunt to collect colours, words, and images. The magic happens when these ideas intersect and you discover new sensations, associations, and meanings.

For many of you, this may be the first time you have ever embarked on any sort of creative project. That's great! You're about to discover how creative you are — and how much fun it is to play. Use the opportunity to explore how silk, lace, and other components of lingerie can influence your mood and behaviour. Let's get started!

GET A JOURNAL: You can buy one or make your own. Visit your local art, office, or stationery store. Whether you decide to use a simple notebook or something more elaborate, let your senses be your guide. What appeals to you? Ideally, your journal should be small enough to carry around with you and big enough to allow you to think and dream freely.

CREATE YOUR COVER: Call it *My Lingerie Journal*. On the first page, write, "This journal belongs to . . ." and fill in your name. Own it! And be creative. Cut out letters from a magazine, use your calligraphy skills, stitch or write your name on a piece of fabric and glue it to the page, or print your name using one or several fonts.

PHOTO: Add a photo of yourself, or kick-start your creativity by drawing a contour selfie! To make a contour drawing, try sketching without lifting your pencil or looking at the piece of paper. Draw from a photo or in front of a mirror. The aim is not to produce a realistic piece of art, but rather to engage in the power of observation. To draw you have to see, and to see you have to look.

Copy the following sections into your journal and answer.

1. What does lingerie mean to you?
2. Is today a good lingerie day?
3. Are you happy with your lingerie selection?

THREE WORDS:

Choose three words that best describe your personality. (For example: independent, generous, good-natured, loyal, traditional, passionate, playful, romantic, sensitive.)

Pick three words that best describe your lingerie preferences. (For example: classic, luxurious, glamorous, provocative, elegant, girly, cheeky, discreet, modern.)

THREE BRAS:

Remember describing your first bra back in chapter 2? Do the same with the bra you're wearing right now. Write down any details that come to mind. Colour? Style? Where did you buy it? Who was with you? How does it make you feel?

Describe two other bras and the memories you associate with them. If possible, try comparing a bra that brings back pleasant memories with one that doesn't.

INSPIRATION PAGES — INSPIRATION BOARD

If you don't know why you have certain items in your drawer and wish you had others, it's time to take a look at your lingerie narrative. What is it that you want to say? Not sure? That's okay. That's what inspiration boards are for. Let's create one. It will give you a chance to discover the sensations that make your body vibrate. Once arranged, your selection of colours, fabric swatches, and images will tell a captivating tale. Remember, there are absolutely no rules. You don't have to be a designer or artistically gifted in any way to make an inspiration board. That's the beauty of it. All you need is a desire to try and a spoonful of courage.

By creating your inspiration pages, or your inspiration board, you are in the process of changing how you see and feel your body in the space around you. These activities provide an opportunity to see colours, symbols, and patterns that are often missed or camouflaged in the blur of daily life. This will ultimately change and enhance your lingerie experience.

ART SUPPLIES AND MATERIALS

Use your journal pages. If you prefer large surfaces, cut the side off a cardboard box, or find a rigid or cardstock sheet at your local art supplies store. You can use Pinterest or some other digital format if you like; however, the richness of an inspiration board relies on texture. The more you can touch and feel with your hands the better. Don't be afraid of making a mess — it's only your right brain showing off!

If you're a creative person, you'll already have everything you need. If you don't think you are a creative person, that's about to change. Start by saying, "I am about to discover my creative side." Then borrow your kids' colouring pencils, or go to a craft store and buy some. While you're there, pick up markers, a glue stick, paint (watercolours or acrylics), and paintbrushes. Favour variety over quality.

COLLAGE

Start gathering ephemera — the small stuff that people often throw away. Think of wrapping paper, ribbons, postcards, magazines, catalogues, feathers, and fabric swatches. Glue, staple, tape, or sew a selection of ephemera into your journal. Don't second-guess your selection. Collecting ephemera is an opportunity to see the details and interesting parts of things. Trust your instincts and your curiosity.

COLOUR

What's your favourite colour? Answer as if you're five years old again with a brand-new box of crayons in front of you. Which one would you pick?

Now look inside your lingerie drawer. Do you see that colour anywhere? Probably not. Once we pass the age of colouring books, we're conditioned to play it safe, be practical, and buy smart — resulting in a drawer full of black and beige. (Psst. I have a colour confession. For ages, I never noticed colour for longer than it took a traffic light to change. Then, one day, I walked past a window display at Ladurée, the famous French bakery known for its macarons. I don't even like to eat those soft, bite-sized meringue and ganache treats, but I stood, transfixed by the saturated, crazy colours. It made me happy just looking at them, and I am now a colour convert.)

We have Sir Isaac Newton to thank for getting the colour wheel rolling in the early eighteenth century. You may already know this, but if not: here are the basics.

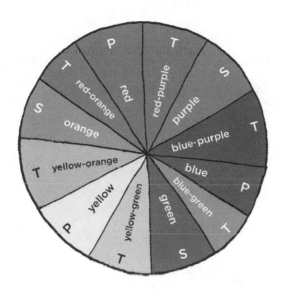

Primary Colours: Red, blue, yellow. These colours cannot be made from mixing other colours.

Secondary Colours: Orange, purple, green. These colours can be created by mixing primary colours together. For example: blue + yellow = green; red + yellow = orange; red + blue - purple.

Tertiary Colours: Hues and shades made from mixing primary and secondary colours.

The way you co-ordinate colours is called a colour scheme. Colour adds interest and vibrancy to every lingerie narrative. Experiment with different colour schemes. Start with the ones suggested on the following pages and then go colour crazy on your own.

Monochromatic: This colour scheme uses tone on tone of the same colour, adding black to darken, or white to lighten. This combo is easy on the eyes, balanced, and elegant in its simplicity. Get out your paints and pick a colour. Draw your own illustrations or trace the one below and add to your journal. Colour in as suggested.

selected colour
selected colour + white
selected colour + black

 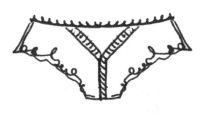

Analogous: The analogous colour scheme uses three colours that are adjacent to each other on the colour wheel. The resulting combination is vibrant, harmonious, and soothing.

Draw your own illustration or trace the one above and add to your journal. Colour and embellish using three analogous colours, for example: red, red-purple, purple or yellow, yellow-orange, orange.

Complementary: This colour scheme uses two colours that sit opposite each other on the colour wheel, such as red and green, or purple and yellow. This combination offers maximum contrast and consequently is dramatic and bold.

Draw your own illustration or trace the one above and add to your journal. Use complementary colours for the bra and panty in one illustration and reverse it in the next. For example: red bra and green panty; green bra and red panty. Also, play with complementary colours as an accent colour for the details.

What colour combinations do you like best? Monochromatic? Analogous? Complementary? Visit your local lingerie boutique and see if you can distinguish the different colour schemes. Describe and/or sketch the window display in your journal. What colour schemes did you see? Inside the boutique, do you notice any consistency between brands and colour schemes?

DETAILS

Here are several ways to explore lace and embroidery details and become more aware of different shapes, patterns, and layers. Take your time and don't worry about the results. Observe the light and shadows as you work and you will begin to understand the expression of sublime.

1. The lace design below is courtesy of the French lace manufacturer Noyon Dentelle in Calais. Scan or make a photocopy of the pattern and put it into your lingerie

journal. Get out your coloured pencils or markers and start colouring carefully in between the lines. Colouring requires a relaxed focus to see the complex patterns; you will find the process remarkably calming as you discover the intricate details.

2. Doodle a detail of your favourite bra. (Don't know how to doodle? Don't worry. Skip ahead to the section on doodles and come back when you're ready.) Take a good look at an embroidery detail or lace pattern while you're having coffee. Do you see the detail more clearly now? Take note of the difference a detail can make both on paper and next to your skin.

3. What lace or embroidery effects do you notice in the ordinary objects and familiar scenes around you? Flowers? Leaves? Curtain patterns? Frost on windowpanes? China patterns? Sketch and/or describe in your journal.

DOODLES

If you don't already doodle, start. It's as calming as it is inspiring. Whether you draw straight lines, curvy lines, circles, squares, or elaborate patterns, every squiggle traces the creativity flowing through you. Lingerie details make for great doodles, and, as all designers know, doodles make great details. Think of it this way: the doodle is in the detail and the detail is in the doodle.

Copy the doodle started here.

Or start your own!

FABRICS

Road trip... to your local fabric store or a vintage clothing store. Look for fabrics that inspire touch. If possible, find fabrics that are in the same range as your colour scheme. Look in the scraps sections of fabric stores, or ask if it's possible to have or buy a sample swatch. If you sew, organize a fabric swap with a couple of friends. If you don't sew, ask a friend who does if you can browse through her scrap pile.

Staple your fabric selection into your journal.

FEEL THE DIFFERENCE

Remember all that hype about active and passive touch in chapter six? Here's a chance to see — I mean *feel* — the difference for yourself. Initially, this exercise might feel forced. It did for me, as if someone asked me to do that thing where you simultaneously rub the top of your head clockwise with your right hand, and rub your stomach counter-clockwise with your left hand. With a little concentration, however, I could distinguish between the two. Understanding the subtle contrasts between active and passive touch will dramatically change how you think about your lingerie and how it feels on your body.

1. Find three panties in your lingerie drawer and lay them out on your bed. Make your selection as diverse as possible; for example, a lace panty, a cotton panty, and a satin panty. If your panties are all 100% cotton, or 100% silk, look for other garments, such as a blouse or a scarf, to add variety.

2. Pick up the first panty and run the fabric through your fingers. Close your eyes to give your full attention. What words come to mind? Soft? Smooth? Stiff? Rough? Rigid? Stretchy? Light? Heavy? Thick? Thin? Scratchy? Is there elastic around the waist? Around the

leg openings? Is there a ruffle? Embroidery? Describe the texture you feel in as much detail as possible. Write down words for comparison with the other textures.

3. Lay the same panty flat down on the bed. Slip your hand through the waist or leg opening so that one layer of fabric is on top of your hand. Close your eyes again to devote your full attention. Describe what you feel. What words or images come to mind? Write them down in your journal. You're developing your own language to identify and define textures.

4. Repeat the same process for the other two panties. Compare the words you used while touching the different fabrics. Observing the differences brings your attention to the texture in a way you may not have noticed before and is an essential step on the way to a greater appreciation of the fabrics and textures used in making lingerie.

5. Next time you are out shopping, stand in front of a clothing rack and run your hands over (actively) and under (passively) clothes. It's interesting to touch and feel how different even seemingly similar fabrics can feel. Rub the fabric between your fingers. Keep your eyes open and then close them. Who cares if anybody notices! Describe the feeling in your journal using as many words or images as come to mind. The more vivid your descriptions and associations, the more you are likely to remember and recall the sensations.

If you can doodle, you can draw.

I love the glamorous and whimsical vibes found in fashion illustrations and have always wanted to learn how to draw like a designer. I asked our illustrator *chérie*, Paloma, if she could show us how. Even if you don't wear French lingerie, you can now draw it! Use tracing paper to copy the outline of the bra and panty. Trace over lightly a couple of times to get a sense of how the shape feels.

BRA:

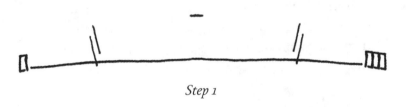

Step 1

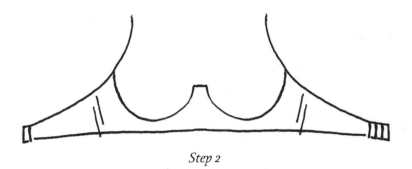

Step 2

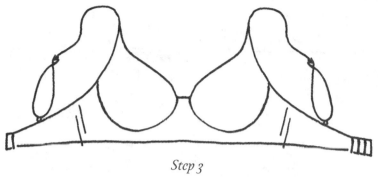

Step 3

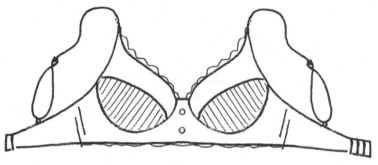

Step 4

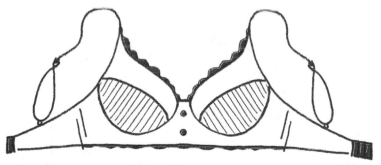

Step 5

Step 1

Step 2

Step 3

The beauty and intrigue of lingerie (and life!) are in the details. Follow these steps to create a lace effect. Not only is it a decorative edge for lingerie, but also for the margins of your journal.

1. Start by drawing a series of half circles. If you're unsure how to start, try using tracing paper.

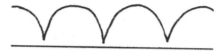

2. Add another row for more dimension. Play with the thickness of your lines to maintain visual interest. Perfection is boring. Variation adds interest.

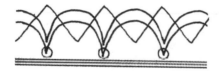

3. Now add a few lines and dots to make a more intricate pattern.

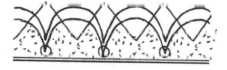

4. Draw a squiggly line above it to complete the edge.

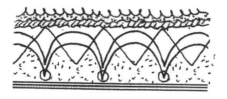

Find a detail (for example, paisley, or a flower or geometric shape) in your favourite bra and sketch it. Like drawing a contour selfie, look at the detail and not at your hand or the paper. By paying attention to the detail, your mind guides your hand. You'll be surprised how effectively you capture the movement and feeling of the detail with this technique.

Copy the grid below and fill it with assorted details. Perhaps you have a bra or panty that you no longer wear? Remove a piece of the trim, take off a ribbon, or cut out a piece of the pattern and glue it in one of the squares in your journal. Then draw it in another one (without looking at your hand!).

In art and fashion, the artistry — and the story — is in the layers. Artists and designers both know how important it is to juxtapose the expected and unexpected. Contrary to popular belief, a layer can't really be covered up. Once it has been created, it exists, even if it isn't entirely visible. The time and effort that went into creating that layer turned into an experience (and hopefully a pleasant one)! It's something to consider the next time you pull on any ole bra and panty. The experience can never be undone — ever.

The following activities illustrate the sensations and visual effects of layering.

Draw a picture frame the size of a page in your journal and fill it with bits of fabric, scrap paper, newsprint, and torn pages from an old magazine or book. Arrange your collage of materials. Experiment with transparency by placing a layer of tissue paper or tracing paper over a piece of fabric or torn pages. See how the texture and the reflection of light changes? Glue, staple, or sew your collage together. Using a coloured pencil, marker, or paint, draw lines or shapes on top of the tissue paper or tracing paper. Even this small detail adds another layer and changes what we see again. If you have some glitter nail polish, add that! Now you have a topcoat of sparkle.

Look at your collage. The juxtaposition of shapes, colours, and textures creates new images and new dimensions. It is through these abstract and random associations that we often see most clearly.

Look at your collage again in a few days. What do you see now? Run your fingers over the surface. What do you remember from the experience?

If you feel really daring, take some black paint and paint over the entire collage. No matter how many layers you had, you can never make it disappear. It's there and always will be, along with your memory of creating it.

SEDUCTION, SEXUALITY, SENSUALITY

You knew it was coming.

What does *seduction* mean to you? What colours does the word evoke? What fabrics? Pick a selection of fabrics that embody and express *seduction* to you.

What do *sexuality*, and, more importantly, *sexy* mean to you? What colours do the words evoke? What fabrics? Pick a selection of fabrics that embody and express sexy to you.

What does *sensuality* mean to you? What colours do the words evoke? Pick a selection of fabrics that embody and express *sensuality* to you.

If you find yourself repeating clichés, don't worry. We have been listening to platitudes for decades, so this is part of the process.

Next time you're in a lingerie store, or flipping through a catalogue, take a moment to look at any merchandising or advertising campaigns. What words are used in what context and with what images? Do they in any way reflect your own selection of words and textures?

SENSES & SENSATIONS

Write down the five senses: sight, sound, smell, taste, and touch. What is each one telling you right now? What do you see? Hear? Smell? Taste? Feel? Describe each sensation as clearly as possible. There are no wrong answers. Clarity and meaning will come when words, colours, doodles, and drawings begin to intersect.

TEXTURES

Texture refers to the surface and tactile quality of a material. Words like *soft, hard, smooth, rough, wet,* and *dry* describe how a texture feels if touched. It's disproportionately more complicated — and insightful — the other way around: using texture to express words.

Let me explain.

Think of a word that describes the texture of organic cotton. *Soft,* for example. Now think of a texture that expresses the word *soft.* Organic cotton, of course, but fur, marshmallows, and velour are possibilities, too. Different people will come up with a different list of words and textures. While there will be crossover and similarities, words mean different things to different people (as suggested in the section "Words").

Think of words in terms of the lingerie vernacular and lingerie textures. This is how the industry works. Designers create prototypes that are then manufactured. The marketing and sales departments at those companies want to sell as many of those designs as possible, and they come up with advertising campaigns using visuals and words to sell lingerie. *Sexy* and *hot* are recurrent words and themes. There is a collective and cultural understanding of what *sexy* means, and a pile of pink and turquoise satin panties to support it. Sexy = satin (texture). But what if satin isn't *sexy* for you? What if *sexy* is a different texture? You might not have thought about the word *sexy* like that before, but felt somehow disconnected and uncomfortable with certain products, and perhaps even not sexy because of it. That's why it is imperative to revisit frequently used words and textures in an industry saturated with innuendo.

Let's try it with other words. Look back at the three words you selected at the beginning of this section to describe your personality. What textures would you select to express those words?

Copy the grid below and fill in the boxes.

personality/texture	ie. romantic/diaphonous	ie. playful/crotcheted

Do the same for the words you used to describe your lingerie preference. What textures would you select to express those words?

Copy the grid below and fill in the boxes.

lingerie preference/texture	ie. glamorous/lustrous	ie. modern/metallic

Look at the different words used to describe textures in both grids. What do you see? Are any of the textures that describe your personality the same as the textures you selected for your lingerie preference? Take time to consider the relationship between both. I find it a compelling narrative whether there are similarities and/or contrasts. Remember, there are no right or wrong answers here, only discovery and exploration.

Next time you are looking at lingerie, pay particular attention to the words used to describe and promote it. Maybe you identify with some of the words and textures; maybe you don't. This awareness is paramount to understanding the choices you have to express yourself.

Sometimes a word can seem so familiar. We know the meaning, but do we know what it means to *us*? Consider words such as *beauty*, *life*, *love*, *joy*, *dreams*, *freedom*, *art* — and, of course, *lingerie*. Browse online for relevant quotes and sayings. A simple word can trigger a memory or an experience so that you can give it more consideration. You should be drawn to the words and feel a certain curiosity even if you're not sure why. Discovering *why* is part of the process.

Select several words, or a quote. Vary the size of the lettering and play with the shapes of the letters. Write your words on lines in your journal — right-side up, right-side down, and sideways!

B
E
A
U
T
Y

LINGERIE

Dreams are necessary for Life. — Anaïs Nin

Look through the pages of your whole journal. Is there a particular theme? There doesn't have to be, although certain words and colour associations have likely appeared. Perhaps you have an untapped passion for pink and purple, eclectic prints, muted elegance, or a sea of calming blues and greens. What discoveries did you make? What words, colours, revelations, sensations surprised you?

In a world of increasing and expected instant gratification, we rely less on ourselves and more on others for fulfillment. Take a moment every day with your lingerie journal. Trust the process. It's a way to remember and appreciate the infinite wonder and satisfaction within each of us.

SIXTEEN

INSIDE YOUR LINGERIE DRAWER

There, all is but order and beauty, luxury, quiet and delight. — Charles Baudelaire

It's time to go through your lingerie drawer. Trust me when I say I've seen everything. At one time my own drawer wasn't so much a lingerie drawer as a holding cell for castaways once they'd been rounded up from the four corners of the bedroom. Back then, BC (Before Caring), my lingerie disappointed me, and I had a feeling that I disappointed my lingerie, resulting in a mutually destructive dynamic.

As you go through your lingerie drawer, think of yourself as the curator of an art collection. It's a natural extension now that you're the designer of your own femininity and sensuality. Your job of a curator is to discover, love, and collect.

Lingerie de jour (day lingerie, such as bras and panties), *lingerie de nuit* (sleepwear, such as pajamas and nightshirts), and *collants/chaussettes* (hosiery, such as leggings and socks) are the major categories to building your lingerie wardrobe and overseeing your collection.

5 STEPS TO CURATING YOUR LINGERIE COLLECTION

1. **EMPTY YOUR LINGERIE DRAWER.** Completely. Lay out all of your bras, panties, stockings, pantyhose, sleepwear, and loungewear, if you have it. If you don't, put out what you wear when you're relaxing around the house. You'll need everything, including what you're wearing now. If you have laundry in process, go fetch it. After today, your drawer will only be for pieces that feel great and that you like wearing. And by like, I mean *really* like. On a scale of one to ten, consider eight the minimum score for any item to continue taking up residence. Anything less has no business being in your drawer, let alone on your body.

2. **TAKE INVENTORY.** Make a chart in your journal. Create six columns with the following headings. Your page might look something like this:

Item	Description	What I love/hate	Size	Fit	Rating
bra	black molded	over-stretched straps	36B	not great	4
panty	organic cotton boyshorts	floral print	M	amazing	9

Go through every item on your bed and fill in your card. For now, focus on making an accurate account of your current inventory. Here are some different scenarios you may encounter:

a) It's a brand-new bra that you've never worn. You feel like you should wear it, but you don't like it. It's been in your drawer for three years. *Au revoir.*

b) The bra was a gift from someone who never really understood you and you never wear it for that reason. *Au revoir.*

c) A lovely bra that you have worn a couple of times — for special occasions only. *Bonjour, bonjour!* And you're going to wear it even more!

d) A bra that you bought (it was on sale!) hoping it would fit if you lost ten pounds, but a) you never lost the ten pounds, or b) you lost the ten pounds and it still doesn't fit. *Au revoir.*

e) A bra and panty set that you had forgotten about. You're thrilled with this discovery and can't wait to wear them again. *Re-bonjour!*

f) It's your everyday beige — oops, I mean "nude" — bra. Practical, and that's it. If practical in your life is worthy of an eight, by all means, keep it. If it makes you feel as blah and invisible as the colour, then you know what to do. Ask yourself the question and listen to your real answer — you'll make the right decision. *Facile.* Easy.

g) Say *au revoir* to those black-and-white panties that have washed out to the same shade, and to the many black leggings and tights with tons of snags and holes. So over.

3. THE FINAL SELECTION. Look closely at what's left. These are the pieces that reflect your personality and in some way bring a smile to your face. Take a minute to decide whether you prefer co-ordinated pieces or if you would rather mix and match according to your own style. In either case, determine how many "sets" you have. Ideally, you will build your collection to include at least eight bras and panties that work together. Eight gives you something to wear on laundry day.

Continue to keep an inventory as you build your lingerie collection. Include the date of purchase and the name of the boutique in your lingerie journal for future reference. Add a doodle of a detail and note the emotions and sensations that come to mind when you wear these pieces. This juxtaposition of words and colour is a record of your insight and appreciation of your lingerie collection.

4. DETERMINE YOUR BUDGET. While luxury lingerie can be expensive, the luxury of wearing lingerie you love doesn't have to be. Make note of your favourite lingerie boutiques and sale periods in order to take advantage of better prices. Buy what you can when you can.

Establishing a budget for lingerie, no matter how big or

small, confirms the importance of lingerie for you so that it becomes a way of life. A budget makes things happen. In business it works like this: More budget, better results. No budget, no results. Remember this about budgets: there is *always* more, if you know where to look. Why not skim/draw from the entertainment budget, for example? You're enjoying your lingerie, *n'est-ce pas*? Include this in your journal.

5. ORGANIZE THE IDEAL DRAWER.

Lingerie de jour

Bras and panties: If you like matching sets, buy two pairs of panties for every bra to get more use out of your bra. If you don't like matching sets, decide how you want to mix and match (by colour? by texture?), and invest in two sports bras if you're active and have the budget. If not, get active, buy one bra, and wash frequently.

Shapewear: If you wear shapewear, you know how fabulous the support and gentle contouring feels. Just make sure there is a design element, too. If there isn't, why not add a Swarovski crystal, rhinestones, or glass beads? There isn't a body out there that doesn't deserve a little sparkle when being squeezed in.

Hosiery: Replace the hosiery that was tossed because of holes. Make one of those purchases a garter belt and a pair of stockings if you've never worn them. Reread chapter 12.

Loungewear: If you still pull on "whatever" after a long day, or wear yoga pants for everything but yoga, it's time for an upgrade. Consider pairing leggings with a full slip, half-slip, or chemise, plus a sweater for comfortable and elegant loungewear. Now would be a good time to say *au revoir* to your alma mater sweatpants.

Lingerie de nuit

Sleepwear is too often overlooked. Preparing your body to rest is an important time of the day. The more relaxed you are, the better you'll sleep. The better you sleep, the better you'll feel. But you already knew that. You just needed a gentle reminder.

Let me also suggest that you have a choice of at least three sleeping options. T-shirts don't count. Take the time to try on pajamas, nightshirts, full slips, camisole, and short sets, all in different fabrics. Do this at a department store or order online and try in the comfort of your home, returning everything if nothing pleases you.

By introducing an evening ritual that includes wearing attractive sleepwear you are preparing both your mind and your body to slow down and unwind, making room for pleasant sensations. Quality sheets are an added benefit for maximum comfort — and are mandatory if you prefer to sleep naked.

Faites de beaux rêves, sweet dreams.

SEVENTEEN

UN JARDIN SECRET

*To know virtue, we must first acquaint
ourselves with vice.* — *Marquis de Sade*

Jardin secret literally translates as "secret garden." It is anything
but the French equivalent of Frances Hodgson Burnett's children's classic *The Secret Garden*, with its cast of orphaned and
crippled children and reverberating promise that love and
goodness will conquer all. For the French, a *jardin secret* is
an area of your life that stays private: a place for your secret
thoughts and desires; a place where being honest with yourself
is what matters most; a whole garden to explore unknown
sensations in your quest to expand and enrich your sensuality
through lingerie.

Sex toys are an obvious choice, especially if you've never
tried them before. If you don't live near a store that sells
vibrators, go online. Online stores are also an excellent how-to
resource and way to catch up on any sex toy vernacular you

might be missing. Remember, however, that while e-learning is a start, experience is the best teacher.

If you are more into drinks than toys with batteries, why not order a glass of champagne in the lobby of a luxury hotel — by yourself. It may be one of the most exhilarating experiences of your life. Hotel lobbies exist in another place and another time. There is freedom to be yourself and someone else at the same time. Watch people. Listen to conversations, read a book, or write a letter. Hotel lobbies are like movie sets and are an excellent backdrop to any story involving secret encounters and lives on the run. It's up to you to decide if you want to cast yourself in the leading role or blend in with the extras. What are you doing tomorrow?

Erotica is another *jardin secret* go-to. Everybody should have a favourite passage or author. If you don't, start googling. This is your chance to see what erotica can or can't do. Do you need things spelled out? Or do you just need a hint of suggestion? Do you like obscure, shocking, or trashy stories? You don't know? Then read a bit of everything.

The following five authors and titles can be found on many French nightstands:

- *Belle de Jour* by Joseph Kessel (or watch the movie with Catherine Deneuve)

- *Delta of Venus* by Anaïs Nin

- *Justine* by Marquis de Sade

- *The Sexual Life of Catherine M.* by Catherine Millet

- *The Story of O* by Pauline Réage

  Bonne lecture, happy reading!

ల

Once you catch your breath, create a section in your journal for your *jardin secret* and consider other areas you might explore. Remember: secrets are fun — it's up to you if you want to keep yours...

I prefer an experimental and accepting *jardin secret*, which is why I signed up for lessons in the art of nipple twirling. Where? At Gentry de Paris's École Supérieure de Burlesque, of course. She taught a *très* popular class, "Make & Twirl Your Own Tassels," and I've included the instructions here.

Make Your Own Tassels

Materials

- soft leather scraps

- glue

- needle and thread

- embroidery thread or ribbon

- tinsel

- glitter glue, sequins, or anything else that sparkles and makes you smile

- double-sided fashion tape — the perfect function for this heretofore faux pas!

(I made my tassels, also called pasties in the burlesque biz, from soft grey leather and covered them with midnight blue and crystal sequins.)

Instructions

Cut a circle out of the leather that is slightly bigger than the diameter of your nipple. Mark the centre and cut a slit from the centre to the edge.

For the tassel, cut equal lengths of tinsel, embroidery thread, or ribbon. Join your threads together and knot. Slide the knotted end through the slit to the centre so that the knot is on the underside of the tassel.

Hold your fingers on either side of the slit and cross over the material slightly to give your disk a cone shape. Stitch together.

Decorate your pasties using glitter glue, sequins, and your imagination.

You're ready to get started!

How to Twirl Your Tassels!

The size and shape of your breasts don't matter if you can get your twirl going.

Keep your back and shoulders straight, and bend your knees slightly.

Trace a figure eight with your hips. Go slowly. Pick up the momentum as you get into the rhythm.

Keep your eyes up and looking out.

The secret to the twirl is in the knees. It's all in the knees.

As for those tassels, remember, what goes around, comes around.

Chin up. Smile. You were born to twirl!

ET VOILÀ

LIFE, LOVE & LINGERIE

I am here to live out loud.
— *Émile Zola*

What began for me as a cultural and linguistic journey — to live in France and learn the language — turned into a delicious lingerie odyssey of self-discovery and awareness.

Most of us struggle with our identity. We create stories about who we are — or think we should be — based on the demands and expectations placed on us by the society and culture in which we live. Too often, our inner selves are not aligned with how we express our outer selves. Lingerie, surprisingly, connects and balances both. When chosen with care and worn with intention, lingerie becomes a subtle layer of what makes you *you*. It is a nurturing and responsive layer of the self that starts on the surface of the skin and radiates both inward and outward. Cultivating good lingerie habits gives you a wardrobe of beauty, but it is also an essential step toward self-confidence and self-love.

At first, the wonder of French lingerie, for me, was that I didn't need to speak French to wear it. But I did need to learn a different kind of language, including body language, to interpret what lingerie had to offer — all the subtleties and feelings and inspiration. Language and lingerie belong together, and I feel the glow and harmony that comes from the presence of both.

It turns out that Paris is the best place in the world to learn the value and promise of lingerie. The romance of love and sensuality is around every corner. You will notice that there's a lot of kissing in Paris. Even the statues kiss. Take a walk through the Rodin sculpture garden, and don't forget the smelling salts should you feel faint from the passion on display. There is something gripping and all-consuming in the way the French love each other — and themselves.

Is it wrong to love yourself too much?

Not at all. According to eighteenth-century philosopher Jean-Jacques Rousseau, there are two kinds of self-love: *amour propre* and *amour de soi*. *Amour propre* is a love for oneself that is motivated by self-interest; a narcissistic love expressed through pride and vanity. *Amour de soi*, on the other hand, is concerned solely with individual well-being and is motivated by a fundamental desire to feel good and care for oneself. It is natural, but must be nurtured. This is the kind of self-love that lingerie can help you build — and it's important, because, too often, this is the kind that is overlooked or neglected. (Interestingly, there are many French lingerie boutiques called *Amour de Soi*, love of self, or *Amour de Soie*, as a play on the French word for silk.)

It's easy to settle into routines and patterns and wrap ourselves in a cocoon of predictability. Lingerie invites us to extend our experience beyond the familiar and into realms of sensory experience, dreams, and possibility.

Learning a foreign language taught me to listen. In the process, I began to hear my body's whispers. This shift in perspective helped me understand lingerie, an area of clothing and life that once held no meaning for me. No longer daunting and abstract, small pieces of fabric prompted greater harmony and peace with my surroundings and myself. Lingerie helped define and enhance the beauty and movement my body offered, and brought freedom, not judgement.

Lingerie is as much about expression as it is about fashion. I hope that this book has helped you think and wear it as a way of expressing yourself inside and out. Use these pages to explore the connection between you, your body, and the world around you.

Lingerie is an invitation to live — and love — your life out loud. In any language.

· V ·

PARIS UNDRESSED

A GUIDE TO LINGERIE SHOPPING IN THE CITY OF LIGHT

❧

French lingerie brands and boutiques to know, and the language you need to enjoy an enhanced lingerie experience

FRENCH BRANDS TO KNOW

A girl should be two things: classy and fabulous.
— *Coco Chanel*

Glamour. Classic. Fashion-forward. Handmade. Chic. Luxury. Erotic.
This selection of French brands shares a commitment to honouring the female form in a range of styles and prices. They are constantly bringing lingerie design to the forefront of fashion, and the results transcend conventional standards of beauty. A new paradigm is evolving, one that celebrates the freedom and expression of femininity in the lingerie of your choice.

Peruse the brands, visit their web sites, and find inspiration in the designs, fabrics, and colour associations. Many of these brands are distributed internationally. Check their web sites for stockists and further information.

Most web sites are in both French and English. Take a look at the French version even if you aren't familiar with the language. It will offer a different perspective from which to explore the potential of your most intimate and sensual side. The French have a wonderful expression, *pour le plaisir des yeux*, which means, for the pleasure of the eyes. Enjoy.

Each brand has been attributed a category to reflect an approximate price range. These categories are to be used as a guideline only. For specific prices, refer to the brand's web site or stockists.

Mid-range: 50€–100€
Premium: 100€–200€
Luxury: 200€–450€
Haute Couture: Custom

ABSOLUTELY PÔM
STYLE: Bold. Urban. Sophisticated.
SPECIALTY: Bras & panties; lifestyle
PRICE RANGE: Luxury
WEB SITE: www.absolutelypom.com
Created in 2009, this spirited brand bursts with style and adventure. Designs reflect a nomadic curiosity and echo an appreciation of different cultures and fabric combinations. From bodysuits and dresses to *nuisettes* and shorts, Absolutely Pôm can be worn day or night, underneath or over top.

AUBADE
STYLE: Creative. Modern. Extravagant.
SPECIALTY: Bras & panties
PRICE RANGE: Premium
WEB SITE: www.aubade.fr
Aubade, which means "dawn serenade" in French, was created in 1875 and is still renowned for its ongoing "Lessons in Seduction" marketing campaign (see chapter 3). Audacious combinations of lace, prints, embroidery, bows, and ribbons produce vibrant collections saturated with colour and emotion.

BARBARA

STYLE: Discreet. Elegant. Innovative.
SPECIALTY: Bras & panties
PRICE RANGE: Premium
WEB SITE: www.barbara.fr

Barbara has been in the business of lingerie since 1926. A forerunner in using stretch lace, the brand continues to seek innovative fabrics and technologies to push design and comfort boundaries. Women feel a familiarity and accessibility with Barbara, which is reflected in their marketing slogan, *Barbara, c'est moi!* Barbara, that's me!

CADOLLE

STYLE: Timeless. Elegant. Luxurious.
SPECIALTY: Bras & panties; made-to-measure
PRICE RANGE: Luxury & haute couture
WEB SITE: www.cadolle.fr

Generations of daughters have continued Herminie Cadolle's legacy that began in 1889 with the invention of the bra. Today, this excellence and expertise is combined with new technology and innovative fabrics so generations of women to come can continue to express their sensuality and freedom through impeccable fit and finesse.

CERVIN

STYLE: Glamour. Seduction. Retro.
SPECIALTY: Garter belts & stockings
PRICE RANGE: Mid-range
WEB SITE: www.cervin-store.com

Dedicated to beautiful legs, Cervin has been manufacturing stockings since 1918 — the real kind that require a garter belt to wear, which they design, too. The art of making and wearing fully-fashioned stockings is known to few but available to all looking for an intimate pause to transcend the day.

CHANTAL THOMASS

STYLE: Chic. Decadent. Irreverent.
SPECIALTY: Bras & panties
PRICE RANGE: Luxury
WEB SITE: www.chantalthomass.com

In the 1970s, Chantal Thomass's keen eye and cheeky designs awakened a nascent desire in women wanting to express themselves through lingerie. She launched her eponymous brand in 1975 and continues to design collections that are intrepid, extravagant, and without apology. With tailored or ruffled details, every collection echoes confidence.

CHANTELLE

STYLE: Classic. Contemporary. Refined.
SPECIALTY: Bras & panties
PRICE RANGE: Premium
WEB SITE: www.chantelle.com

A family-owned company founded in 1876, Chantelle's collections reflect years of expertise and craftsmanship. Committed to innovation, Chantelle is recognized for creating the first two-way stretch fabric in 1878 that revolutionized the market and opened new possibilities for elasticized fabrics. Purity of form resonates throughout the collections, bringing classic elegance to contemporary designs.

ELISE ANDEREGG

STYLE: Sophisticated. Elegant. Feminine.
SPECIALTY: Lifestyle
PRICE RANGE: Luxury
WEB SITE: www.eliseanderegg.com

Elise designed her first collection in 2004 and immediately established her signature style of lingerie-to-wear in the spirit of ready-to-wear. Light but not fragile fabrics and materials create contemporary silhouettes with timeless elegance.

ELISE AUCOUTURIER
STYLE: Modern. Elegant. Fashion-forward.
SPECIALTY: Bras & panties; lifestyle
PRICE RANGE: Luxury
WEB SITE: www.eliseaucouturier.com
Created in 2001, this brand takes an untraditional approach to lingerie, challenging colour and textile associations to surprising effect. Diaphanous lace with contrasting threads, fabrics, and textures create intrigue and alternately conceal or reveal the beauty of the female body.

EMPREINTE
STYLE: Quality. Elegant. Refined.
SPECIALTY: Bras & panties
PRICE RANGE: Premium
WEB SITE: www.empreinte.eu
The name Empreinte comes from the French song, "*Je ne peux effacer l'empreinte du passé*," meaning "I can't erase the imprint of the past." Created in 1946, this exacting and alluring brand designs for generous busts. Carefully selected fabrics and attention to detail reveal Empreinte's dedication to shaping and outlining contours with finesse and impeccable support.

ERES
STYLE: Minimal. Pure. Contemporary.
SPECIALTY: Bras & panties
PRICE RANGE: Luxury
WEB SITE: www.eres.fr
In 1968, designer Irène Leroux revolutionized the swimwear industry by declaring swimsuit season all-year round, not just for the summer, and sculpted women's bodies with impeccable fabrics and design. In 1998, Eres launched its first lingerie collection and once again illustrated the art of the body with shrewd cuts and innovative fabrics.

FIFI CHACHNIL

STYLE: Pink. Girly. Polka dots.

SPECIALTY: Bras & panties

PRICE RANGE: Luxury

WEB SITE: www.fifichachnil.com

Fifi loves pink, from the palest to the most vibrant shade, and her designs embody the softness and strength of femininity. Full of romanticism, her retro-glam collection of bras, bloomers, and baby dolls is made of silk, lace, and tulle. Where there's a frill, there's a thrill.

GERMAINE DES PRÉS

STYLE: Modern. Natural. Colourful.

SPECIALTY: Lifestyle

PRICE RANGE: Mid-range

WEB SITE: www.germainedespres.com

A more recent brand, created in 2011, Germaine des Prés specializes in versatile designs made in natural fabrics (cotton voile) that cross over effortlessly from day to night. Romantic styles in saturated colours reflect the spirit of this liberated and fashionable lifestyle brand.

HUIT

STYLE: Fashion-forward. Creative. Chic.

SPECIALTY: Bras & panties

PRICE RANGE: Mid-range

WEB SITE: www.huit.com

Huit is French for the number eight, which, observed vertically, resembles the sensual contours of the female form. Horizontally, it represents the sign of infinity and suggests the outline of a woman's breasts. Created in 1968, this fashion-driven brand appeals to young women looking for stylish expression in a modern world.

IMPLICITE

STYLE: Glamorous. Edgy. Graphical.

SPECIALTY: Bras & panties

PRICE RANGE: Mid-range

WEB SITE: www.implicite-lingerie.fr

Implicite means "implied" or "understood." As the name suggests, this brand offers a stylistic identity for smart women looking for passion and a little trouble. Launched by the Simone Pérèle group in 2007, Implicite combines glamour, elegance, and mystery. Contemporary cuts and daring embroidery are used to extraordinary graphic effects.

JOLIES MÔMES

STYLE: Romantic. Colourful. Exquisite.

SPECIALTY: Bras & panties

PRICE RANGE: Luxury

WEB SITE: www.joliesmomes.com

Jolies mômes doesn't just mean pretty girls. It suggests a spirited woman playful in her femininity. Inspired by the freedom of the 1970s and Woodstock, collections are designed to reflect harmony and luminosity through the luxury of selected fabrics. Each piece is handmade and numbered.

LES JUPONS DE TESS

STYLE: Provocative. Erotic. Elegant.

SPECIALTY: Bras & panties

PRICE RANGE: Luxury

WEB SITE: www.lesjuponsdetess.com

Founded in 2007, Les Jupons de Tess, meaning "Tess's Petticoats," heralds the beauty and allure of the eighteenth century and the life of a courtesan. An ode to femininity, styles reflect indulgent desires, and carefully selected materials move with the body and its pleasures.

LINGERIE DEMENT
STYLE: Playful. Daring. Surprising.
SPECIALTY: Bras & panties
PRICE RANGE: Luxury
WEB SITE: www.lingerie-dement.com
Dement is a play on the words *dément/démential,* meaning "wild," and *amant/aimant*, meaning "lover" and "magnet." Founded in 2010, this brand creates and satisfies insatiable desire. Magnetic attraction literally holds everything together as small magnets are sewn underneath bows to be flicked and released on a whim.

LISE CHARMEL
STYLE: Opulent. Sophisticated. Elegant.
SPECIALTY: Bras & panties
PRICE RANGE: Luxury
WEB SITE: www.lisecharmel.com
Dating back to the 1950s, Lise Charmel's creativity and expertise captures the extravagance of luxury. Nourished by references to French and Italian art, the brand has created a singular identity through elaborate designs layered with lavishly saturated colour and exquisite embroideries.

LOU PARIS
STYLE: Spirited. Hip. Elegant.
SPECIALTY: Bras & panties
PRICE RANGE: Premium
WEB SITE: www.loulingerie.com
Lou was born out of love — literally. Boy (André) meets girl (Lucienne) on the Orient Express, and in 1946 they created the brand that has become Lou Paris. With an eye toward fashion for inspiration and styling, Lou's collections offer contemporary designs in a luminous colour palette.

MA P'TITE CULOTTE
STYLE: Spirited. Humorous. Character.
SPECIALTY: Bras & panties; lifestyle
PRICE RANGE: Mid-range
WEB SITE: www.maptiteculotte.com

Launched in 2013, this young brand creates lingerie with style and humour, with particular attention and affection given to panties. *Ma P'tite Culotte* means "my small panty" in French, suggesting familiarity over size. The abbreviated *p'tite*, for petite, adds character. Fabric quality and softness is of the utmost importance, and every effort is made to finding the best weavers.

MADAME AIME
STYLE: Timeless. Elegant. Chic.
SPECIALTY: Bras & panties
PRICE RANGE: Luxury
WEB SITE: www.madame-aime.com

Founded in 2014, Madame Aime is a fashion-forward lifestyle brand designed by bra experts. Sculptural and graphic, this brand combines couture details and a saturated colour palette for a modern and feminine silhouette.

MAISON CLOSE
STYLE: Erotic. Chic. Free.
SPECIALTY: Bras & panties
PRICE RANGE: Premium
WEB SITE: www.maison-close.com

Inspired by the *belle époque* and an era of libertinism, Maison Close embodies the allure and freedom of seduction. Since its creation in 2006, Maison Close has challenged the codes and perception of nudity. More than a brand, Maison Close is a philosophy and lifestyle focused on desire and subtle defiance.

MAISON LEJABY

STYLE: Chic. Elegant. Alluring.
SPECIALTY: Bras & panties
PRICE RANGE: Premium
WEB SITE: www.maisonlejaby.com

A hallmark of French lingerie that can be traced back to 1884, Lejaby was officially founded in 1930. Fashion-forward and innovative, the company was a forerunner in Lycra usage, imbuing its collections with an ultra-chic silhouette and divine comfort. Always feminine, Maison Lejaby combines lustrous fabrics and colours to stunning effects.

MARJOLAINE

STYLE: Silk. Lace. Finesse.
SPECIALTY: Lifestyle
PRICE RANGE: Luxury
WEB SITE: www.marjolaine.fr

Marjolaine has been a family-owned business since 1947, and lace incrustation is its signature. Incrustation is the meticulous process of cutting lace by hand and sewing it to the garment so that the threads follow the curves of the lace. Contrasting colours of silk and lace cascade over the body and intrigue dances in the shadows.

MAUD & MARJORIE

STYLE: Contemporary. Fashion-forward. Chic.
SPECIALTY: Bras & panties
PRICE RANGE: Premium
WEB SITE: www.maudandmarjorie.com

Design-focused Maud Juillard and Marjorie Collard revisited lingerie and swimwear codes and created a new style that is modern, tailored, and designed to sculpt the body. Careful attention is given to ensure the precise cutting of patterns and fabrics in order to maintain soft, whimsical, yet graphic lines.

OCCIDENTE

STYLE: Versatile. Eco. Modern.

SPECIALTY: Lifestyle

PRICE RANGE: Premium

WEB SITE: www.occidente-boutique.fr

Founded in 2008, occidente specializes in ecological and ethically sourced collections that reflect a commitment to well-being, design, nature, and fair trade. In a range of muted colours, the collection is easy to mix and match and crosses over from lingerie to eveningwear, or yoga wear to daywear, to complement your choice of fashion and lifestyle.

ODILE DE CHANGY

STYLE: Romantic. Lace. Retro.

SPECIALTY: Bras & panties

PRICE RANGE: Luxury

WEB SITE: www.odiledechangy.fr

What would you do if you found a drawer full of exquisite underpinnings in your family chateau? If you were Odile de Changy, you would become a lingerie designer and create romantic and delicate collections with a taste of nostalgia. Each piece is made from luxurious silks and laces and embodies the independent spirit of women of the past and the poetry of today.

PALOMA CASILE

STYLE: Black. Lace. Chic.

SPECIALTY: Bras & panties

PRICE RANGE: Luxury

WEB SITE: www.palomacasile.com

Paloma created her eponymous brand in 2012 with unparalleled provocation and style. From triangle bras to full-length lace bodysuits, Paloma's collections dare. Her designs are as graphic, modern, and sensual as her illustrations throughout this book.

PRINCESSE TAM TAM

STYLE: Fashion-forward. Playful. Refined.

SPECIALTY: Bras & panties

PRICE RANGE: Mid-range

WEB SITE: www.princessetamtam.com

Princesse tam tam was founded in 1985 and named after the 1935 film of the same name, starring Josephine Baker. This is a vibrant and dynamic brand, where choice of colour palette, delightful prints, and soft fabrics infuse confidence and charm for an easy, natural elegance.

SIMONE PÉRÈLE

STYLE: Elegant. Sophisticated. Refined.

SPECIALTY: Bras & panties

PRICE RANGE: Premium

WEB SITE: www.simone-perele.com

A celebration and expression of femininity and timeless elegance, this brand continues to embody the sophistication that first inspired a young, independent, and spirited couturier named Simone Pérèle in 1948. Exceptional fabrics and attention to detail combine beauty and comfort in an uncompromising aesthetic and fit.

VANNINA VESPERINI

STYLE: Fashion-forward. Vibrant. Elegant.

SPECIALTY: Lifestyle

PRICE RANGE: Luxury

WEB SITE: www.vanninavesperini.com

If dreams are in colour, designer Vannina Vesperini must dream in Technicolor. Created in 1996, Vannina Vesperini quickly became recognized for designs featuring vibrant silks and lace. Vannina is one of the pioneers of lingerie-to-wear, and her camisoles easily cross over from daywear to eveningwear, or from summer to winter.

YSÉ

STYLE: Modern. Natural. Delicate.
SPECIALTY: Bras & panties
PRICE RANGE: Premium
WEB SITE: www.yse-lingerie.com

The smaller the better: Ysé specializes in A and B cups. Equal parts fashion and lingerie, the fabrics include Calais lace, chiffon, and microfibre. With a tendency toward the avant-garde, Yse's simple and elegant designs offer a sensuality often lacking in the smaller sizes.

PARISIAN LINGERIE BOUTIQUES

Luxury is not a necessity to me, but beautiful
and good things are. — Anaïs Nin

You've climbed the Eiffel Tower, strolled through the Tuileries, marvelled in front of Notre Dame, splashed in the Stravinsky Fountain, posed next to *The Thinker*, and drifted down the Seine in a *bateau mouche*.

But have you cinched a Cadolle corset around your waist? Slipped into a breathtaking Carine Gilson silk chemise? Flirted in the femininity of a Fifi Chachnil charmeuse panty, or savoured the modern purity of Eres? It would be a mistake to leave Paris without taking a look at your silhouette *undressed* in Aubade, Cadolle, Chantal Thomass, Lise Charmel, or Simone Pérèle. Discover the lingerie temples of Paris. Don't just linger in front of the window. Push the door open and treat yourself to that *ooh la la* feeling that only French lingerie can provide.

Paris is a shopper's paradise, with many areas recognized for their allure and selection. While many of the lingerie brands are in the same area as fashion houses, several designers have their showrooms and ateliers off the beaten track. A list of lingerie boutiques and itineraries follows. While some brands have their own stores, others don't. If a brand cited in the previous section is not mentioned here then it does not have a stand-alone store in Paris, at least for now, while some brands have several locations. Check web sites to find other locations and for a complete list of independent retailers. These itineraries have been co-ordinated to group several stores together in a specific area you might be interested in visiting. Of course, it's always fun to create your own itinerary and discover un-expected surprises and delights along the way.

CONCORDE/MADELEINE/HAUSSMANN

AUBADE
23, rue Tronchet
75008 Paris
+33 (0)1 42 66 53 97
METRO: Madeleine
WEB SITE: www.aubade.fr
* Visit Aubade's web site for a complete list of boutiques.
A boudoir-style boutique presenting the brand's bold mix of prints, colours, fabrics, and accessories.

EMPREINTE
13, rue Saint-Florentin
75008 Paris
+33 (0)1 42 61 71 78
METRO: Concorde
WEB SITE: www.empreinte.eu
Empreinte offers a confidential setting for the plus-size market. In their uniquely designed L'Atelier Lingerie, clients can select their own embellishments and even request to have their initials embroidered in their purchases.

ERES
2, rue Tronchet
75008 Paris
+33 (0)1 47 42 28 82
METRO: Concorde
WEB SITE: www.eres.fr
*Visit the Eres web site for a complete list of boutiques.
The minimalist decor of the boutique reflects the modern yet timeless design of Eres's luxurious lingerie and swimwear collections.

GALERIES LAFAYETTE
40, boulevard Haussmann
75009 Paris
+33 (0)1 42 82 34 56
METRO: Havre–Caumartin
WEB SITE: www.galerieslafayette.com
Recognized worldwide, the department store Galeries Lafayette offers a vast range of lingerie and hosiery.

LA PERLA
20, rue du Faubourg Saint-Honoré
75008 Paris
+33 (0)1 43 12 33 60
METRO: Concorde
WEB SITE: www.laperla.com
*Visit La Perla's web site for a complete list of boutiques.
An Italian brand renowned for elegance and refinement.

PRINTEMPS
64, boulevard Haussmann
75009 Paris
+33 (0)1 42 82 50 00
METRO: Havre–Caumartin
WEB SITE: www.departmentstoreparis.printemps.com
This department store has recently been renovated and includes
major brands and designer labels in a sophisticated setting.

CAMBON/SAINT-HONORÉ

AGENT PROVOCATEUR
12, rue Cambon
75001 Paris
+33 (0)1 42 61 79 54
METRO: Concorde
WEB SITE: www.agentprovacateur.com
*Visit Agent Provocateur's web site for a complete list of boutiques.
A British brand with international appeal that is elegantly designed
for deliberate incitement.

CADOLLE
4, rue Cambon
75001 Paris
+33 (0)1 42 60 94 22
METRO: Concorde
WEB SITE: www.cadolle.fr
A Parisian institution designing made-to-measure luxury lingerie
since 1889.

CHANTAL THOMASS
211, rue Saint-Honoré
75001 Paris
+33 (0)1 42 60 40 56
METRO: Tuileries
WEB SITE: www.chantalthomass.com
The chic boutique of French designer and icon Chantal Thomass —
daring, feminine, and always elegant.

FIFI CHACHNIL
68, rue Jean-Jacques Rousseau
75001 Paris
+33 (0)1 42 21 19 93
METRO: Louvre–Rivoli
WEB SITE: www.fifichachnil.com
* Visit Fifi Chachnil's web site for a complete list of boutiques.
A sweet, retro, and frilly boudoir for this delightful brand.

PALOMA CASILE
10, rue du Jour
75001 Paris
+33 (0) 6 50 51 49 71
METRO: Louvre–Rivoli
WEB SITE: www.palomacasile.com
The atelier, design studio, showroom, and boutique for the designer's
daring and ultra-glamorous collections.

LE MARAIS

AUBADE
33, rue des Francs Bourgeois
75004 Paris
+33 (0) 1 42 76 96 87
METRO: Saint-Paul
WEB SITE: www.aubade.fr
* See description on page 204 and visit Aubade's web site for a complete list of boutiques.

DOLLHOUSE
27, rue du Roi de Sicile
75004 Paris
+33 (0)1 40 27 09 21
METRO: Saint-Paul
WEB SITE: www.dollhouse.fr
A two-floored boutique with a collection of provocative lingerie and
a selection of sex toys.

ODILE DE CHANGY
6, rue du Pont aux Choux
75003 Paris
+33 (0)1 42 78 86 25
METRO: Saint-Sebastien–Froissart
WEB SITE: www.odiledechangy.fr
The boutique and atelier for Odile's delightful collections, which are
reminiscent of the past.

PRINCESSE TAM TAM
29, rue des Francs Bourgeois
75004 Paris
+33 (0)1 44 78 96 21
METRO: Saint-Paul
WEB SITE: www.princessetamtam.com
*Visit princesse tam tam's web site for a complete list of boutiques.
Trendy and feminine collections presented in a warm and relaxed
atmosphere.

SIMONE PÉRÈLE
84, rue François Miron
75004 Paris
+33 (0)1 42 76 92 25
METRO: Saint-Paul
WEB SITE: www.simone-perele.com
A recently opened boutique, representing the brand's distinctive
style and expertise.

YSÉ
117, rue Vieille du Temple
75003 Paris
+33 (0)1 42 74 22 71
METRO: Filles du Calvaire
WEB SITE: www.yse-lingerie.com
This boutique reflects the simplicity and elegance of a brand dedicated
to small bust sizes.

SAINT-GERMAIN-DES-PRÈS

AGENT PROVOCATEUR
38, rue de Grenelle
75007 Paris
+33 (0)1 45 49 09 44
METRO: Sèvres–Babylone; Rue du Bac
WEB SITE: www.agentprovocateur.com
* See description on page 220 and visit Agent Provocateur's web site for a complete list of boutiques.

CARINE GILSON
18, rue de Grenelle
75007 Paris
+33 (0)1 43 26 46 71
METRO: Sèvres–Babylone; Rue du Bac
WEB SITE: www.carinegilson.com
An exquisite boutique and showroom for this Belgian designer's refined collection of luxurious silks and laces.

EMILIA COSI
20, rue Saint-Sulpice
75006 Paris
+33 (0)1 43 54 78 66
METRO: Odéon
WEB SITE: www.emiliacosi.com
A luxury lingerie boutique with a striking range and selection of brands.

ERES
4, bis rue du Cherche-Midi
75006 Paris
+33 (0)1 45 44 95 54
METRO: Sèvres–Babylone
WEB SITE: www.eres.fr
* See description on page 207 and visit Eres's web site for a complete list of boutiques.

FIFI CHACHNIL
34, rue de Grenelle
75007 Paris
+33 (0)1 42 22 08 23
metro: Sèvres–Babylone; Rue du Bac
web site: www.fifichachnil.com
* See description on page 208 and visit Fifi Chachnil's web site for a complete list of boutiques.

IMPLICITE
4, rue de Babylone
75007 Paris
+33 (0)1 45 49 94 54
metro: Sèvres–Babylone
web site: www. implicite-lingerie.fr
A modern boutique for this modern brand that showcases the collections of contemporary, colourful, and graphic designs.

LISE CHARMEL
7, rue du Cherche-Midi
75006 Paris
+33 (0)1 42 22 63 93
metro: Sèvres–Babylone; Saint-Sulpice
web site: www.lisecharmel.com
Lise Charmel recently opened a Parisian boutique in a magnificent and luxurious *hôtel particulier*, mansion, to welcome clients and showcase collections.

PRINCESSE TAM TAM
4, rue de Sèvres
75006 Paris
+33 (0)1 45 48 27 49
metro: Sèvres–Babylone
web site: princessetamtam.com
* See description on page 214 and visit princesse tam tam's web site for a complete list of boutiques.

SABBIA ROSA
73, rue des Saints Pères
75006 Paris
+33 (0)1 45 48 88 37
METRO: Saint-Germain-des-Près
Sabbia Rosa opened in 1976, and Monnette Moati personally curates her boutique devoted to luxurious silk lingerie, notably camisoles and nightgowns in stunning colours.

LE BON MARCHÉ
24, rue de Sèvres
75007 Paris
+33 (0)1 44 39 80 00
METRO: Sèvres–Babylone
WEB SITE: www.lebonmarche.com
A preferred department store of Parisians with a refined and sophisticated lingerie department.

PASSY

ERES
6, rue Guichard
75016 Paris
+33 (0)1 46 47 45 21
METRO: La Muette
WEB SITE: www.eres.fr
* See description on page 207 and visit Eres's web site for a complete list of boutiques.

PRINCESSE TAM TAM
4, rue Guichard
76016 Paris
+33 (0)1 45 24 55 96
METRO: La Muette
WEB SITE: princessetamtam.com
* See description on page 214 and visit princesse tam tam's web site for a complete list of boutiques.

MONCEAU

AUBADE
93, rue de Courcelles
75017 Paris
+33 (0)1 46 22 55 27
METRO: Courcelles
WEB SITE: www.aubade.fr
* See description on page 204 and visit Aubade's web site for a complete list of boutiques.

LOUISE FEUILLÈRE
102, rue des Dames
75017 Paris
+33 (0)1 42 93 17 76
By appointment only.
METRO: Villiers; Rome
WEB SITE: www.louisefeuillere.com
Made-to-measure lingerie that includes camisoles, corsets, nightgowns, bras, and panties.

JUST OUTSIDE OF PARIS

NUITS DE SATIN
156, boulevard du Général de Gaulle
92380 Garches
+33 (0)1 47 95 44 17
By appointment only.
TRAIN STATION: Garches–Marnes-La-Coquette
WEB SITE: www.nuitsdesatin.com
A showroom displaying a vast collection of vintage lingerie, including swimwear and corsets from the nineteenth century.

VANNINA VESPERINI
16, passage de la Gêole 1er étage
78000 Versailles
+33 (0)9 52 74 63 43
METRO: Versailles Rive Droite
WEB SITE: www.vanninavesperini.com
A boutique and showroom for bold, colourful silk and lace lingerie.

THE LANGUAGE OF
LINGERIE

A special kind of beauty exists which is born in language, of
language, and for language.
— Gaston Bachelard

More than a glossary, the language of lingerie explores the
relationship between words, emotions, and textures. In some
cases, it isn't the exact definition of a word that is interesting,
but rather its meaning, interpretation, and connection and
relationship to lingerie. The words and expressions that follow
have been selected based on their ability to inspire, expand,
and enhance your lingerie experience.

À FLEUR DE PEAU French expression meaning "very close to the
surface of the skin."

ADHESIVE BRA A stick-on bra to be worn only when all else fails.

AESTHETIC Awareness and heightened appreciation of beauty.

ALLURE To entice, charm, attract.

AMOUR French for "love"; it should be shared generously.

ART DE VIVRE The art of living; a way of being and thinking.

AU REVOIR French for "goodbye." Courtesy tip: learn it and use it every time you leave a store.

BALCONETTE A style of bra where the cups have less height, covering the bottom half of the breast, and giving a straight bustline. Straps are wider set.

BAMBOO A natural plant fibre.

BAND The base of the bra that goes around the rib cage.

BANDEAU A strapless style of bra or bathing suit that wraps around the breasts.

BASQUE A long, contour-fitting bodice that is less rigid than a corset. See also *guêpière*.

BELLE ÉPOQUE A period of prosperity and prestige in France, stretching from the late nineteenth century to the beginning of World War I.

BIAS A diagonal line to the grain of the fabric that when cut gives garments a flattering, draping effect over the body.

BIEN DANS SA PEAU A French expression meaning "to feel good in one's skin" or "to feel good about oneself."

BIKINI A style of panty that sits well below the waist with high-cut leg holes.

BODY An exquisite structure of bones and flesh that showcases and gives movement to lingerie.

BONJOUR French for "hello." Learn it and use it every time you go into a store.

BOUDOIR A private dressing room.

BOXER A short-shaped panty style that covers both the hips and buttocks.

BOYSHORT A mid-rise panty style that almost covers the buttocks. Referred to as a "shorty" in French.

BRA A breast-supporting garment that women spend their lifetime trying to figure out. See also *brassiere*.

BRA EXTENDER A little piece of extra bra strap that hooks on to your bra closure to lengthen the band.

BRA PAD A pad (usually made from foam or gel) to wear underneath your bra to accentuate the volume of your breasts.

BRASSIERE A French word originally used to describe a boy's undershirt that was picked up in America in the early twentieth century to describe the new craze of breast-supporting garments. Over the years, it was shortened to *bra*.

BRIEF Considered the classic panty style; can be high- or low-waisted, but provides full coverage, front and back.

BUSTIER A close-fitting garment similar in design to a corset but shorter and less constricting. With its built-in bra, a bustier boosts and accentuates the bust rather than flattening it.

CALAIS A city in northern France where Leavers lace originated in the nineteenth century. The manufacturing of *dentelle de Calais*, lace of Calais, continues today using the same machines, techniques, and expertise, passed on from generation to generation.

CAMAÏEU A range of tones in the same colour.

CAMISOLE A delicate sleeveless top made of light fabric and often trimmed in lace.

CARE LABEL Effective cleaning and care instructions based on the fibre composition of a textile garment. Follow them.

CENTRE FRONT The fabric between the cups of a bra. Also referred to as the *centre gore*.

CHAMPAGNE A sparkling white wine produced in Champagne, a region in northeast France. Tastes great with all lingerie.

CHEMISE A longer-styled shirt or slip made of delicate fabrics, such as silk or cotton, and often trimmed in lace and embellished with decorative details.

CLASSIC PANTY This style of panty can be high- or low-waisted, but provides full coverage, front and back. Also referred to as a *brief*.

CLEAVAGE The space between the breasts: the smaller the space, the bigger the cleavage.

CLOSURE The spot where the front of the bra meets the back — or vice versa. The most frequently used closure is a hook and eye.

COLOUR Shades, tones, and hues resulting from absorbed and reflected light. Appreciated in the beauty and glory of a rainbow and too often absent in lingerie drawers.

COMFORTABLE Something that provides a feeling of well-being.

CONTOURS The gentle curves that outline a woman's silhouette.

CORSELET-GORGE The name of the two-piece corset introduced at the World's Fair in Paris in 1889 by Herminie Cadolle, who is recognized as a pioneer of the modern bra.

CORSET A fitted garment that laces up tightly and shapes the torso by defining the waist, hips, and breasts.

COTTON A soft natural fibre composed mostly of cellulose.

CUBAN A style of stocking recognized by the vertical, rectangular design on the heel.

CULOTTE French for "panty."

CUP The part of the bra that cradles, supports, and shapes the breast.

CURIOSITY A desire to explore and discover — essential for nourishing all the senses.

CUT-AND-SEW BRA A bra cup that is made up of two or three pieces that are sewn together, creating seams that help lift, control, and shape.

DÉCOLLETÉ French for "low neckline."

DÉCOLLETÉ DE RÊVE French expression for "a beautiful bustline."

DELICATE A fine, soft, subtle pleasing of the senses.

DEMI CUP A bra style that is cut on the diagonal, covering half to three-quarters of the breast.

DENIER The weight in grams of 9,000 metres of fibre or yarn.

DENTELLE French for "lace."

DÉPAREILLÉ French for "mismatched." In the context of lingerie, it means your bra doesn't match your panties, which is all good — if you did it on purpose, of course.

DESSOUS French for "below," or "under." *Les dessous* is a French expression for "undergarments."

DIAPHANOUS Translucent; letting some light through, but not completely transparent.

DRAPE The manner in which fabric hangs.

DREAM Images, feelings, and sensations that occur while we're sleeping or awake. Both are essential.

EIFFEL TOWER An iron structure over 300 metres high that was designed by Gustave Eiffel and built for the 1889 exposition in Paris; it is now a national symbol and landmark. It has been suggested that the intricate metalwork of the Eiffel Tower represents lace, while the four pedestals act as the clips on a garter belt.

ÉVEILLER LES SENS A French expression meaning "to awaken the senses," which is what good lingerie does.

ELASTANE The generic name for a synthetic fibre of great elasticity. Known as *spandex* in America.

ELASTICITY The ability of a material to recover its original shape after stretching.

ELEGANT Timeless. Always comfortable. Always chic.

EMBROIDERY Decorative needlework applied to fabric using thread and a variety of different embellishments.

EMOTION A strong feeling that creates a sensation. Notice both.

EXTRAORDINARY Something different that makes an experience unforgettable. So much better than ordinary.

FABRIC A cloth made by knitting, weaving, or felting fibres.

FASHION A certain style or way of dressing that is popular during a particular period.

FAUX PAS Uh-oh.

FIBRE A natural or synthetic filament that can be spun into threads and yarns.

FLAX A plant fibre used for the production of linen.

FLOSSING Decorative embroidery.

FRAME The base of the bra where the cups sit. Also known as the *cradle*.

FRENCH POINT A style of stocking with an elongated and delicate design that comes to a point just above the heel.

FROU-FROU A French word to express an abundance of lace, ribbons, bows, and frilly textures.

FULL CUP A bra style that covers the whole breast.

FULLY-FASHIONED STOCKINGS Stockings that are knitted flat and sewn together at the back.

GARTER BELT A garment that attaches around the waist with clips to attach and hold up stockings.

GRANDE BOURGEOISIE A socio-economic term used to denote the upper class.

GUÊPIÈRE An all-in-one bra, bustier, and garter belt.

GUIPURE Often called *open lace*, guipure is really embroidery produced by stitching patterns on a fabric background that is then chemically dissolved, leaving only the pattern.

HALF CUP Another term for "demi cup," which is a bra style cut on the diagonal and covering half to three-quarters of the breast.

HAUTE COUTURE Exclusive designer fashion at stratospheric prices.

HAVANA A style of stocking with a short and wide rectangular design on the heel.

HIGH-CUT PANTY A full-coverage panty often referred to as "granny panties."

HIPSTER A low-rise panty style in between a bikini and boyshorts that sits on the hips.

HOLD-UPS A type of stocking that can be worn without a garter belt. Made with an elasticized band to keep them in place. Also known as *stay-ups*.

HOSIERY The general term for any legwear such as stockings, pantyhose, tights, or nylons.

IMAGINATION The ability to dream and create.

IMPERFECTION A beautiful and unique characteristic that can be mistakenly referred to as a flaw.

INSPIRE To stir deeply.

INTRIGUE Of interest and fascination — essential to consider when selecting lingerie.

ITALIAN PANTY A luxurious full-coverage panty with high-cut legs and transparent mesh sections.

JACQUARD A weaving loom invented by Joseph Jacquard (1752–1834) that operated with a system of perforated cards for guiding threads. Once adapted to lace making, any pattern was possible, and the lace making industry exploded.

JARDIN SECRET A French expression that translates to "secret garden" and refers to a private place for your thoughts and desires.

JERSEY A type of knitted fabric that hugs the body.

JOIE DE VIVRE A French expression suggesting an inherent love and zest for life.

KEYHOLE The shape on the back of a fully-fashioned stocking that forms during the manufacturing process. Once the stocking has been knitted flat and sewn together, the top of the stocking is folded down over itself to create a double layer, which creates a finishing loop in the shape of a keyhole.

KNITTED FABRIC A fabric composed of interconnecting loops, providing good stretch and recovery.

LACE An openwork fabric of fine threads.

LASER CUT A process that allows synthetic fabrics to be cut with extreme heat that also seals any edges, so there are no unravelling threads, or bulky seams.

LASTEX A yarn with an elastic core used in stretch fabrics.

LAYERS A combination of overlapping textures that creates enhanced visual effects and sensations.

LEAVERS Lace woven on a Leavers loom that produces intricate patterns. This is the only kind of lace that is made up out of warp and weft. All other laces are knitted.

LINGERIE A collection of undergarments that are worn based on their ability to trigger or provide extraordinary sensations.

LINGERIE DE JOUR The French term for undergarments worn during the day.

LINGERIE DE NUIT The French term for elegant sleepwear.

LOUNGEWEAR The term used for elegant casual clothing.

LYCRA A brand name for *elastane* and *spandex*.

LYOCELL A type of rayon fibre made from cellulose.

MADE-TO-MEASURE An item that is custom-made for you and only you.

MANHATTAN A style of stocking with a decorative outline around a pointed, elongated design on the heel.

MASS MARKET Something made for you — and everybody else.

MICROFIBRE An extremely fine synthetic fibre that is very smooth and molds to the body when blended with stretchable fibres, such as elastane.

MINIMIZER BRA A bra that reduces the bust line by flattening the breasts.

MOCK-SEAMED A stocking where the seam has been added on to resemble a fully-fashioned stocking.

MODAL A regenerated fibre that is made from beechwood using chemical processing.

MOLDED BRA A bra with a seamless pre-formed cup.

NATURAL FIBRES Fine threads that come directly from plants and animals; can be twisted into yarn.

NEW LOOK Christian Dior's silhouette that celebrated a return to glamour and all things feminine, including slim waists and defined breasts.

NIPPLE COVERS Small round or petal-shaped adhesive Band-Aids for sensitive or shy nipples.

NIPPLE TASSELS Party clothes for not-so-shy nipples.

NUDE BRA Sold as the perfect solution for every occasion, this bra will inspire zero stories to tell your grandchildren.

NUISETTE An above-the-knee nightgown.

NYLON A synthetic fibre and fabric that is renowned for its strength and resilience.

ORDINARY Regular. Uninteresting. A missed opportunity when associated with lingerie.

ORGANZA A lightweight, transparent, stiff woven fabric usually made from silk or synthetic fibres.

PANTY Functions as underwear, serves as body art.

PARIS The lingerie capital of the world. It's in France.

PASTIES A decorative nipple cover in interesting shapes and textures, and usually covered in sequins.

PLAISIR French for "pleasure." A feeling or source of delight.

PLUNGE A style of bra that has a lower centre front, which increases cleavage and provides support for fashions with low necklines.

POLYAMIDE A term for "nylon" used in Europe.

POLYESTER A synthetic fibre and also a fabric.

PORTE-JARRETELLES French word for "garter belt."

POUR LE PLAISIR DES YEUX French expression meaning "for the pleasure of the eyes."

PUSH-UP A bra style with angled cups to push breasts in for more cleavage and up for more volume.

QUALITY An accumulation of details, including better materials and more labour, to make something the best. Often undervalued or disregarded in a world that celebrates fast and disposable.

RAYON A manufactured fibre composed of regenerated cellulose.

REGENERATED FIBRES Fine threads that are part natural and part chemical.

RÊVERIE A daydream.

RHT A term applied to stockings to indicate a reinforced heel and toe.

SALE A price discount. Overused in marketing to incite purchasing. Never the only reason to buy something.

SATIN A soft, shiny fabric.

SAVOIR FAIRE Excellence born from expertise and passion.

SCALLOPED EDGES A decorative, half-circle shape used as a finishing detail on fabrics.

SEAMLESS Undergarments that are made using technology other than stitching to avoid visible lines.

SENSUALITY The beauty and mystery that lies in the space between modesty and provocation.

SEXY Overtly suggestive of sex. Often imbued with judgement regarding sartorial choices and behaviour. Overused in lingerie marketing.

SHAPEWEAR Garments made with a high degree of spandex to smooth and shape contours of the body.

SHORTY The French term for "boy short"; a mid-rise panty style that that almost covers the buttocks.

SHOULDER PADS Silicone cushions to protect your skin from chafing beneath your bra strap.

SILHOUETTE The outline or shape of a body.

SILK A soft, shiny fibre spun by silkworms during their metamorphosis and obtained from their cocoon.

SISTER SIZES Refers to the same volume, or cup size, that can be found in a different bra size.

SOUTIEN-GORGE (SOUTIF) Literally translates to "throat support," and is the French for "bra." It first appeared in the Larousse dictionary in 1904. The slang for *soutien-gorge* is *soutif.*

SPANDEX The generic name for a synthetic fibre of great elasticity. Spandex is the term used in North America; *elastane*, the other generic word, is used elsewhere in the world.

SPECIAL OCCASION A predicted time and reason to celebrate. In the past, one of the reasons you might have decided to wear lingerie.

SPLURGE Considered overspending for everything but lingerie.

SPORTS BRA A bra designed to cut down breast motion during physical activity, which can reduce pain and future sagging.

STAY-UPS A type of stocking that is held up with silicone bands instead of a garter belt. Also know as *hold-ups.*

STOCKINGS A woven or knit fabric that covers the foot and legs and requires a garter belt to be held up. To be tried at least once in a lifetime.

STRAP A narrow piece of fabric or elastic that goes over the shoulder to attach the top of the bra cup to the back band.

STRAPLESS BRA A style of bra without straps, which is often worn under backless fashions.

SUBLIME Inspiring wonder and awe.

SYNTHETIC A manufactured product formed through a combination of chemicals.

SYNTHETIC FIBRES Fine threads that are 100% chemically engineered.

T-SHIRT BRA A bra with smooth cups to conceal nipple definition; marketed to wear under tight-fitting garments.

TAILLE DE GUÊPE French expression for "wasp waist" that is used to define very small waists created with corsets and *guêpières*.

TANGA A triangle shaped panty with high-cut legs and a low-cut waist.

TAPE Often used for giftwrapping and sometimes used to hold down wayward fabrics.

TEXTURE A quality of surface. Intrinsic to fabric choices and sense of touch.

THONG Half a tanga.

TREND A general direction or tendency. For fashionistas, it's what's in vogue. In lingerie, trends are fun, but not the defining factor.

TRIANGLE BRA A bra in the form of a triangle that covers the breasts but doesn't provide any support.

TOUCH One of the most important senses when it comes to lingerie.

TULLE A light, transparent fabric made from silk or cotton.

UNDERWEAR A word you might have used in the past to describe your bra and pantics. Now, of course, you wear *lingerie*.

UNDERWIRE A U-shaped metal support sewn into the base of the bra cup for additional reinforcement and shaping. You know you're wearing the best when you set off metal detectors at airports.

VISCOSE A generic term for fibre composed of regenerated cellulose. Synonymous with *rayon*.

VULGAR Lacking in refinement. Poor taste. Crude. Beautiful lingerie is never vulgar.

WARP Vertical threads in a woven fabric.

WASPIE A waist cincher that comes with or without garter straps.

WEAVE The crossover of warp and weft threads.

WEFT Horizontal threads in a woven fabric.

WELT The darker band on the top of a stocking.

WING The part of a bra between the cups and the closure.

WOOL A natural animal fibre.

WOVEN Fabrics that are made by weaving two yarns together at right angles. Technically speaking, it is the crossing of weft threads (horizontal) over or under warp threads (vertical).

ACKNOWLEDGEMENTS

What a thrill it is to share this page in the privileged company of those who helped me find the language and expression for *Paris Undressed*. In their honour, I have opened a bottle of champagne. Please join me in raising a glass in celebration.

To Jami Bernard at Barncat Publishing for guiding me with wit and unwavering patience from my first written word on June 4, 2007, to my last page. Every writer deserves you in their corner. Your vision and clarity aside, the best part of all this has been walking beside you as your friend.

To Anita Bryant and Melissa Crabbins for your committment to being kind yet honest readers week after week and year after year.

To Meredith Dees, for seeing something more in this manuscript and taking a risk despite resistance from one very uncertain writer. This book is better because of you.

To Sarah MacLachlan and the entire team at House of Anansi for undertaking this unique project.

To Paloma Casile for the delightful illustrations and pouring your soul and talent into everything you make.

To Madame Annabelle, Gentry de Paris, Ghislaine Rayer, and Julia Palombe for sharing the secrets of your sensuality and showing me how to have fun with mine.

To Stéphane de Bourgies for my author photo and for capturing a black-and-white moment in time.

To all the lingerie designers for their passion and graciously sharing their creativity and knowledge.

To Olivier Noyon for providing exquisite Leavers lace samples from the archives of Noyon Dentelle.

To Docteur Thierry Leonard for your wisdom and gentle kindness.

To Briony, Owen, Sinclair, Mackenzie, and Fiona for being the best cheerleading squad.

And to Christian, for being there to help me get dressed and undressed.

Merci.

KATHRYN KEMP-GRIFFIN is a journalist and entrepreneur. She has been living in Paris and working in the lingerie industry since 1990. She started her own lingerie company, Soyelle, which specialized in accessories and beauty products, before founding Paris Lingerie Tours — the ultimate luxury rendezvous for helping women fulfill their lingerie dreams. In 2009, she founded Pink Bra Bazaar, a charitable organization dedicated to breast health education and supporting women with breast cancer. Born in Canada, she lives in an old millhouse outside of Paris with her husband, five children, and assorted pets.

PALOMA CASILE designs an eponymous line of lingerie. She graduated top of her class from ESMOD Paris, the oldest fashion school in the world. She apprenticed in houses such as Chantal Thomass and Cadolle before winning the lingerie prize at the Dinard Festival of Young Fashion Designers. She lives in Paris.